THE YOUNG PHILOSOPHER'S GUIDE

EXPLORING LIFE'S BIG QUESTIONS

DR. MINAKSHI BANSAL

DEDICATION

*To the young philosophers of today and tomorrow,
whose curiosity, wonder, and passion for knowledge
will shape the world.*

𐑀𐑀𐑀

Contents

Contents

Contents

Prayer

"Om Bhadram Karnebhih Shrinuyama Devah

Bhadram Pashyemakshabhiryajatrah

Sthirairangais Tushtuvamsastanubhih

Vyashema Devahitam Yadayuh

Svasti Na Indro Vriddhashravah

Svasti Nah Pusha Vishwavedah

Svasti Nastarkshyo Arishtanemih

Svasti No Brihaspatir Dadhatu

Om Shantih Shantih Shantih"

This mantra is a prayer for universal well-being, invoking the blessings of various deities for protection, health, and happiness. It emphasizes the importance of experiencing the auspicious through all senses and living a life aligned with divine purpose. The repetition of "Shantih" at the end signifies a deep desire for peace in the individual, the environment, and the universe at large. This mantra is often recited as a prayer for peace, prosperity, and the physical and spiritual well-being of all beings.

▷▷▷

About The Author

This book represents the culmination of extensive research and meticulous analysis, incorporating a diverse range of sources, including numerous books, scholarly studies, and personal experiences. Additionally, I have scoured various websites to gather relevant information and data essential for the compilation of this work. I have taken every precaution to ensure the accuracy of the information presented and have diligently cited all sources to acknowledge their contributions.

From her earliest days, Minakshi was distinguished by an insatiable appetite for reading. Her literary universe was inhabited by characters and narratives that spanned ethical tales, motivational and inspirational stories, and the mythic parables imbued with life lessons. This voracious reading habit was not merely for personal edification but was driven by a desire to distill and disseminate the essence of these narratives to foster the development of students and peers alike. She was particularly captivated by the lives and teachings of historical figures and spiritual leaders such as Adi Shankaracharya, Swami Vivekananda, Dr. APJ Abdul Kalam, Mahamana Pandit Madan Mohan Malviya, Mahatma Gandhi, Sardar Vallabhai Patel, and Vinoba Bhave, among others. Their philosophies and life stories fueled her ambition to embody their ideals of resilience, selflessness, and relentless pursuit of knowledge.

Dr. Minakshi's academic and practical engagement with psychology has been equally noteworthy. As a research scholar, her focus has been on exploring the intricate tapestry of the human psyche, aiming to unlock the potential for psychological well-being and societal harmony. Her scholarly work is complemented by her active involvement in social work, where she employs her academic insights to make tangible differences in the lives of the underprivileged. Her endeavours in social work are characterized by an innovative approach that combines traditional wisdom with contemporary psychological practices to address the multifaceted challenges faced by these communities.

Her artistic talents, another facet of her diverse capabilities, are not merely a personal passion but also serve as a medium through which she communicates and connects with others. Her art, rich in symbolism and emotional depth, reflects her philosophical inquiries and social concerns, offering viewers a glimpse into the breadth of her intellect and the depth of her compassion.

In addition to her contributions to the arts and social sciences, Dr. Minakshi has embraced the healing arts of Pranic Healing, mastering the techniques developed by Master Choa Kok Sui. This practice, which focuses on the manipulation of Prana or life energy to heal the body and aura, has been both a personal journey of discovery and a means through which she extends her healing touch to others. Her proficiency in Pranic Healing is complemented by her advocacy and teaching of various forms of meditation aimed at rejuvenation, personal betterment, and the cultivation of harmony within individuals and communities alike.

Dr. Minakshi's life is a narrative of relentless pursuit, not just of personal achievement but of the upliftment and empowerment of society at large. Her diverse interests and talents—spanning the arts, literature, psychology, and the healing practices—converge on a singular path of service. She embodies the spirit of the luminaries who inspired her, channelling their legacy through her actions and teachings. Through her books, art, and social initiatives, she continues to inspire a new generation to embark on their own journeys of self-discovery, resilience, and altruism.

Her commitment to social betterment, particularly her focus on uplifting underprivileged children, reflects a deep understanding of the transformative potential of education and personal development. By integrating her knowledge of psychology, her artistic sensibilities, and her healing practices, Dr. Bansal has developed a holistic approach to social work that addresses both the immediate needs and the long-term well-being of the communities she serves.

As an author, Dr. Minakshi's writings offer a blend of inspirational insights, practical wisdom, and reflective contemplations drawn from her extensive reading and life experiences. Her books serve as a guide for those seeking to navigate the complexities of life with grace, resilience, and purpose. Through her narratives, she extends an invitation to her readers to explore the depths of their own potential and to contribute meaningfully to the collective well-being of society.

In Dr. Minakshi Bansal, we find a remarkable synthesis of the artist, the scholar, the healer, and the social activist. Her life's work stands as a beacon of hope and a source of inspiration for individuals seeking to make a difference in the world. Her story is a compelling reminder of the power of individual action, rooted in compassion and driven by a profound commitment to the betterment of humanity. Dr. Minakshi's legacy is not just in the tangible outcomes of her efforts but in the enduring spirit of inquiry, empathy, and service that she embodies.

ppp

Preface

In the tapestry of human existence, questions are the threads that weave together our understanding of ourselves, the world around us, and the mysteries that lie beyond. The young mind, with its insatiable curiosity and unbridled wonder, is particularly adept at asking these profound questions. "Why am I here?" "What is the meaning of life?" "Is there a right and wrong?" These inquiries, often dismissed as childish musings, are in fact, the seeds of philosophical inquiry, the very foundation of our quest for knowledge and wisdom.

In this book, we invite you, the young philosopher, to embark on an extraordinary journey of exploration and discovery. Together, we will delve into some of life's most profound and perplexing questions, seeking to unravel their complexities, challenge our assumptions, and expand our understanding of the world and our place in it.

This is not a book that offers easy answers or definitive solutions. It is a guide, a companion, a catalyst for critical thinking and open-minded inquiry. It is an invitation to embrace the power of questions, to engage in thoughtful dialogue, and to explore the diverse perspectives that have shaped human thought throughout history.

We will journey through the realms of philosophy, science, and the human experience, exploring questions about the nature of reality, the meaning of life, the existence of God, the origins of the universe, the power of love, the value of art, and the future of humanity. We will encounter a rich tapestry of ideas, from ancient wisdom traditions to cutting-edge scientific discoveries, from philosophical debates to artistic expressions.

Along the way, we will encounter some of the greatest thinkers and philosophers of all time, from Plato and Aristotle to Descartes and Kant. We will learn about their ideas, their arguments, and their contributions to our understanding of the world. But we will also challenge their assumptions, question their conclusions, and develop our own unique perspectives.

This book is not just about learning new facts or memorizing theories. It is about developing critical thinking skills, honing our ability to analyze arguments, and forming our own informed opinions. It is about cultivating a lifelong love of learning, a thirst for knowledge, and a passion for exploring the mysteries of life.

This book is for the curious, the inquisitive, and the open-minded. It is for those who are not afraid to ask questions, to challenge the status quo, and to seek out new perspectives. It is for those who believe that the pursuit of knowledge is not just an intellectual exercise, but a journey of self-discovery and personal growth.

In this book, we will not shy away from difficult or controversial questions. We will grapple with issues of morality, ethics, and social justice. We will explore the complex relationship between faith and reason, science and spirituality, freedom and responsibility. We will confront the challenges of our time, such as climate change, inequality, and political polarization, and we will consider our role in shaping a better future.

This book is not just for young people. It is for anyone who is curious about the world and their place in it. It is for those who are seeking to deepen their understanding of themselves and others, to find meaning and purpose in their lives, and to make a positive impact on the world.

In the end, this book is about more than just answering questions. It is about embracing the power of inquiry, the joy of discovery, and the transformative potential of ideas. It is about cultivating a lifelong love of learning, a passion for exploration, and a commitment to making the world a better place.

Dr. Minakshi Bansal
Social Activist
Ahmedabad, Gujarat, Bharat

❦❦❦

ONE

WHAT IS REAL? DELVING INTO THE NATURE OF REALITY.

What is real? This is a question that has puzzled philosophers, scientists, and thinkers for centuries. It's a question that young minds are especially primed to ponder, as they begin to explore the world around them and try to make sense of their experiences. The nature of reality is a vast and complex topic, but we can embark on an exciting journey to explore some key ideas and concepts that can help us understand this fundamental question.

Our senses tell us that the world is solid, tangible, and real. We can see the trees, feel the wind on our skin, and taste the sweetness of an apple. But are our senses always reliable? Sometimes our eyes can be deceived by optical illusions, and our ears can mishear sounds. So, how can we be sure that what we perceive is an accurate representation of reality?

Philosophers have debated this question for centuries, and many different theories have emerged. One influential idea is that there are two distinct realms of reality: the physical world and the world of ideas. The physical world is the world we experience through our senses, while the world of ideas is a realm of abstract concepts and principles that exist independently of the physical world.

Plato, a famous Greek philosopher, believed that the world of ideas was more real than the physical world. He argued that the physical world is constantly changing and decaying, while the world of ideas is eternal and unchanging.

For Plato, the physical world is like a shadow or reflection of the more fundamental reality of the world of ideas.

Other philosophers, like René Descartes, have questioned the very existence of the physical world. Descartes famously wondered whether he could be certain of anything at all, even his own existence. He concluded that the only thing he could be certain of was his own thinking.

This led him to the famous statement, "I think, therefore I am." Descartes' philosophy raises the possibility that our entire experience of the physical world could be an illusion.

But even if the physical world is real, what is it made of? Scientists have been trying to answer this question for centuries, and their investigations have led to some fascinating discoveries. We now know that the physical world is made up of tiny particles called atoms, which are themselves made up of even smaller particles. These particles are constantly in motion, interacting with each other in complex ways.

The discoveries of modern physics have also challenged our traditional understanding of space and time. Einstein's theory of relativity tells us that space and time are not absolute but are relative to the observer.

This means that time can pass at different rates for different observers depending on their relative motion. It also means that gravity can warp the fabric of space and time, creating strange phenomena like black holes.

Another important aspect of reality is consciousness. What is consciousness, and how does it arise from the physical world? This is one of the most perplexing mysteries of science and philosophy. Some scientists believe that consciousness is simply a product of the brain, while others believe that it is something more fundamental that cannot be reduced to physical processes.

One intriguing idea is that consciousness is not limited to the brain but is a property of the universe itself. This idea, known as panpsychism, suggests that even inanimate objects like rocks and trees may possess some degree of consciousness.

While this may sound far-fetched, some scientists believe that panpsychism could help explain some of the mysteries of consciousness.

Another aspect of reality that is often overlooked is the role of the observer. Quantum mechanics, the theory that describes the behavior of subatomic particles, tells us that the act of observation can affect the outcome of an experiment. This has led some physicists to propose that consciousness may play a fundamental role in the structure of reality itself.

Of course, these are just a few of the many ideas and theories that have been proposed about the nature of reality. It's a topic that is likely to continue to fascinate and challenge us for many years to come. What is real?

The answer to this question may ultimately depend on our own individual perspectives and beliefs. But by exploring the different ideas and theories that have been proposed, we can gain a deeper understanding of ourselves and the world around us.

As young philosophers, it's important to remember that there are no easy answers to these big questions. But by asking these questions and seeking out different perspectives, we can expand our minds and deepen our understanding of the world. Remember, the journey of exploring reality is just as important as the destination.

❧❧❧

Reality is a kaleidoscope of interpretations, each shaped by our unique perspectives and experiences. What is real to one may be illusion to another. The pursuit of truth is an endless journey, guided by curiosity and open-mindedness.

TWO

WHO AM I? UNRAVELING THE MYSTERY OF IDENTITY.

Who am I? This is a question that has echoed through the ages, whispered in moments of quiet reflection and shouted in times of crisis. It's a question that philosophers, poets, and artists have grappled with, seeking to understand the fundamental nature of our existence and our place in the world. As young philosophers, we too embark on this journey of self-discovery, seeking to unravel the mystery of our identity.

At first glance, the answer to this question may seem obvious. We are individuals, each with our own unique name, physical appearance, and personality traits. But is this all there is to us? Are we simply a collection of physical and psychological attributes? Or is there something deeper, something more essential that defines who we are?

Many philosophers have argued that our identity is shaped by our experiences, relationships, and social roles. We are daughters and sons, sisters and brothers, friends and lovers. We are students, athletes, artists, or perhaps future scientists or philosophers. These roles and relationships shape our values, beliefs, and aspirations, and they contribute to our sense of self.

But is our identity fixed and unchanging? Or is it something that evolves and transforms over time? Many philosophers believe that our identity is dynamic and fluid, constantly shaped and reshaped by our experiences and interactions with the world. We are not the same person we were yesterday, and we will not be the same person tomorrow.

Some philosophers argue that our identity is rooted in our consciousness or our sense of self-awareness. We are aware of our thoughts, feelings, and sensations, and this awareness distinguishes us from inanimate objects and other living beings. Our consciousness allows us to reflect on our past experiences, plan for the future, and make choices that shape our lives.

But what is consciousness? Is it a product of the brain, or is it something more mysterious and elusive? Scientists and philosophers are still trying to understand the nature of consciousness, but many believe that it is a complex phenomenon that emerges from the interactions of countless neurons in the brain.

Another aspect of our identity is our cultural background. We are born into families and communities with their own unique traditions, customs, and beliefs. Our cultural heritage shapes our language, our values, and our worldview. It influences our food preferences, our style of dress, and even our sense of humor. Our cultural identity can be a source of pride and belonging, but it can also be a source of conflict and alienation.

In a world that is becoming increasingly interconnected, our cultural identities are constantly evolving and interacting with other cultures. We are exposed to different ways of life, different values, and different perspectives. This can be a source of enrichment and growth, but it can also be a source of confusion and disorientation. As young philosophers, we must learn to navigate this complex cultural landscape and find our own unique path.

Our identity is also shaped by our individual choices and actions. We are not simply passive recipients of our experiences, but active agents who can shape our own destiny. We can choose to embrace new challenges, pursue our passions, and make a difference in the world. Our choices and actions reflect our values, our beliefs, and our aspirations, and they contribute to our sense of self.

But are we truly free to choose our own path? Or are our choices determined by forces beyond our control? Some philosophers argue that our choices are ultimately determined by our genes, our upbringing, or the social and cultural environment in which we live. Others believe that we have free will, the ability to make choices that are not predetermined by external factors.

The question of free will is a complex and controversial one, but it has important implications for our understanding of identity. If our choices are predetermined, then our sense of agency and responsibility may be illusory. But if we have free will, then we are truly the authors of our own lives, and our identity is shaped by the choices we make.

Ultimately, the question of "Who am I?" is a deeply personal one. There is no single answer that applies to everyone. We each have our own unique journey of self-discovery, shaped by our experiences, relationships, and choices. As young philosophers, we must embrace this journey with curiosity, open-mindedness, and a willingness to explore different perspectives.

Remember, the question of "Who am I?" is not a destination, but a lifelong journey. It is a journey that can lead to greater self-awareness, self-acceptance, and self-actualization. By embracing this journey, we can discover our true potential and live a life that is authentic, meaningful, and fulfilling.

ᐅᐅᐅ

Identity is a tapestry woven with threads of experience, relationships, and choices. We are not fixed entities, but constantly evolving beings, shaped by the world around us and the choices we make. Embrace the journey of self-discovery and unlock your true potential.

THREE

WHY AM I HERE? DISCOVERING PURPOSE AND MEANING.

Why am I here? This profound question echoes in the hearts of countless individuals, young and old alike. It's a question that has fueled philosophical inquiry, religious contemplation, and personal introspection for millennia. As we embark on this journey of self-discovery, we delve into the realm of purpose and meaning, seeking to understand our place in the grand tapestry of existence.

The quest for purpose and meaning is a fundamental human aspiration. We yearn to know that our lives matter, that we are not merely random occurrences in a vast and indifferent universe. We seek a sense of direction, a compass to guide us through the complexities and challenges of life. This quest can take many forms, from pursuing personal passions and goals to seeking spiritual enlightenment or contributing to the betterment of society.

For some, the answer to the question "Why am I here?" lies in religious or spiritual beliefs. Many religions offer a framework for understanding our existence, suggesting that we are here to fulfill a divine plan or purpose. We may be called to serve God, to live a virtuous life, or to spread love and compassion to others. These beliefs can provide a profound sense of meaning and purpose, giving our lives a sense of direction and significance.

Others find meaning and purpose through their relationships with family, friends, and loved ones. We are social beings, wired for connection and belonging. Our relationships with others can provide us with love, support, and a sense of community. They can challenge us to grow, to learn, and to become better versions of ourselves.

For many, our work and careers can also be a source of purpose and meaning. We spend a significant portion of our lives working, and the nature of our work can have a profound impact on our sense of self-worth and fulfillment. Work that allows us to use our talents and skills, to make a difference in the world, and to contribute to something larger than ourselves can be deeply meaningful.

Some individuals find their purpose in creative pursuits, such as art, music, or writing. Creativity allows us to express our unique perspectives, to explore our emotions, and to connect with others on a deeper level. It can be a source of joy, inspiration, and personal growth.

For others, the pursuit of knowledge and understanding can be a lifelong quest for meaning. We are curious beings, eager to learn about the world around us and our place in it. The pursuit of knowledge can lead us to new discoveries, new perspectives, and a deeper appreciation for the complexity and beauty of the universe.

The question of purpose and meaning is not always easy to answer. It can be a lifelong journey of exploration and self-discovery. There may be times when we feel lost or uncertain, questioning our path and our place in the world. These are natural and even necessary parts of the journey. It is through these challenges that we grow, learn, and ultimately discover our true purpose.

It is important to remember that there is no one-size-fits-all answer to the question "Why am I here?" Each of us has our own unique path to follow, our own unique gifts to share with the world. Some of us may find our purpose early in life, while others may take longer to discover it. Some may find that their purpose evolves and changes over time, while others may find a consistent theme throughout their lives.

Ultimately, the most important thing is to be open to the possibilities, to embrace the journey of self-discovery, and to trust that we are here for a reason. We may not always know what that reason is, but by living our lives with intention, curiosity, and compassion, we can create a life that is meaningful and fulfilling.

As young philosophers, we are at a unique stage in our lives, where the world is full of possibilities and opportunities. We have the freedom to explore different paths, to try new things, and to discover our passions. We have the potential to make a positive impact on the world, to contribute to something larger than ourselves.

But with this freedom comes a responsibility to choose wisely, to live our lives with integrity, and to make choices that align with our values and aspirations. We must also be mindful of the impact our choices have on others and on the world around us. By living our lives with purpose and meaning, we can not only fulfill our own potential but also contribute to the betterment of society and the world.

So, why are we here? The answer to this question may ultimately be a mystery, but it is a mystery worth exploring. By embracing the journey of self-discovery, we can unlock our true potential, create a life of purpose and meaning, and make a positive impact on the world.

❧❧❧

The search for meaning and purpose is a fundamental human quest. It is a journey that takes us beyond the mundane and into the realm of values, passions, and contributions to the world. Live a life of intention, embrace your unique gifts, and make a positive impact.

FOUR

IS THERE A RIGHT AND WRONG? EXPLORING THE FOUNDATIONS OF MORALITY.

Is there a right and wrong? This question lies at the heart of morality, a concept that has fascinated philosophers, theologians, and thinkers for centuries. As we embark on this exploration of the foundations of morality, we delve into the complex and often controversial terrain of ethics, seeking to understand what it means to be good, to act justly, and to live a virtuous life.

The question of right and wrong is not merely a theoretical one. It has profound implications for how we live our lives, how we interact with others, and how we shape the world around us. Our moral beliefs guide our actions, shape our relationships, and influence our decisions, both big and small. But where do these moral beliefs come from? Are they universal truths, or are they simply cultural constructs?

One perspective on morality is that it is rooted in human nature. We are social beings, wired for cooperation and empathy. We have an innate sense of fairness and a natural aversion to harming others. This suggests that morality is not something we learn, but something that is inherent in our very being.

Another perspective is that morality is a product of culture and upbringing. We learn from our families, communities, and societies what is considered right and wrong. Our moral values are shaped by the stories we hear, the examples we see, and the lessons we are taught. This suggests that morality is not universal, but varies from culture to culture and from individual to individual.

Philosophers have long debated the nature of morality, and many different theories have emerged. Some, like Immanuel Kant, argue that morality is based on reason and universal principles. We have a duty to act in accordance with these principles, regardless of our personal desires or consequences. Others, like Jeremy Bentham and John Stuart Mill, believe that morality is based on utility and the pursuit of happiness. The right action is the one that produces the greatest amount of happiness for the greatest number of people.

Religious traditions also offer a variety of perspectives on morality. Many religions believe that morality is rooted in divine commands or revelations. We are obligated to follow these commands because they are the will of God or a higher power. Others emphasize the importance of compassion, forgiveness, and love for our fellow human beings.

In recent years, science has also begun to shed light on the origins of morality. Studies in evolutionary biology and neuroscience suggest that morality may have evolved as a way to promote cooperation and social cohesion. Our brains are wired to respond to moral dilemmas, and our emotions play a crucial role in our moral judgments.

But even if we can explain the origins of morality, the question of what is right and wrong remains complex and multifaceted. There are many different moral values, and they often conflict with each other. For example, the value of individual freedom may conflict with the value of social justice. The value of loyalty to one's family may conflict with the value of honesty and integrity.

How do we resolve these conflicts? One approach is to prioritize certain values over others. For example, we may believe that the value of human life is more important than the value of property, or that the value of truth is more important than the value of loyalty. Another approach is to seek a balance between competing values, recognizing that there is no single right answer to every moral dilemma.

The exploration of morality is a lifelong journey. It is a journey that requires us to question our assumptions, to challenge our beliefs, and to engage in open and honest dialogue with others. As we navigate this complex and often challenging terrain, we must be guided by a commitment to truth, compassion, and the pursuit of a just and equitable society.

In our personal lives, we can strive to live in accordance with our values, to treat others with respect and compassion, and to make choices that promote the well-being of ourselves and others. We can also work to create a more just and equitable society by advocating for policies that promote equality, opportunity, and human rights.

As young philosophers, we have a unique opportunity to shape the future of morality. We can challenge outdated and harmful beliefs, promote new and innovative ideas, and contribute to a world that is more just, compassionate, and sustainable. By embracing this challenge, we can create a legacy that will benefit generations to come.

ᏗᏗᏗ

Morality is a compass that guides us through the complexities of right and wrong, fairness and equality. It is a constantly evolving landscape, shaped by our values, beliefs, and experiences. Strive to live a life of integrity, compassion, and justice.

FIVE

WHAT IS THE GOOD LIFE? CONTEMPLATING HAPPINESS AND WELL-BEING.

What is the good life? This question has been pondered by philosophers, theologians, and everyday individuals for centuries. It's a question that speaks to our deepest desires and aspirations, our longing for happiness, fulfillment, and a sense of purpose. As we embark on this contemplation of the good life, we will delve into the complex and often elusive concepts of happiness and well-being, seeking to understand what truly makes a life worth living.

At its core, the good life is a life well-lived. But what does that mean? For some, the good life is synonymous with happiness – a state of joy, contentment, and satisfaction. We seek pleasure, avoid pain, and strive to maximize our positive experiences. This hedonistic view of the good life emphasizes the importance of pursuing pleasure and minimizing suffering, whether through material possessions, social connections, or personal achievements.

However, happiness is a fleeting emotion, often dependent on external circumstances and prone to fluctuations. Can a life solely focused on pursuing pleasure truly be considered good? Many philosophers argue that the good life involves more than just the pursuit of happiness. It involves a deeper sense of meaning, purpose, and fulfillment.

Aristotle, a prominent Greek philosopher, believed that the good life, or eudaimonia, is achieved through the cultivation of virtue and the pursuit of excellence. We are rational beings, and our happiness is tied to our ability to reason well and to live in accordance with our rational nature. This involves developing our character, cultivating good habits, and striving to be the best version of ourselves.

For Aristotle, the good life is not about maximizing pleasure, but about living a virtuous life. This means acting in accordance with moral principles, cultivating good relationships, and contributing to society. It means using our talents and abilities to their fullest potential, and striving to make a positive impact on the world.

Other philosophers have emphasized the importance of relationships and social connections in the good life. We are social beings, and our well-being is deeply intertwined with our connections to others. Meaningful relationships with family, friends, and loved ones can provide us with love, support, and a sense of belonging. They can enrich our lives, challenge us to grow, and help us cope with adversity.

Community engagement and social contribution can also be important aspects of the good life. When we contribute to something larger than ourselves, whether through volunteering, activism, or simply being a good neighbor, we can experience a sense of purpose and meaning that extends beyond our individual lives. We can feel connected to a larger community and contribute to the well-being of others.

Some philosophers emphasize the importance of personal growth and development in the good life. We are constantly evolving and changing beings, and our well-being is tied to our ability to learn, grow, and adapt to new challenges. The pursuit of knowledge, skills, and experiences can enrich our lives, broaden our perspectives, and help us reach our full potential.

Creativity and self-expression can also play an important role in the good life. Whether through art, music, writing, or other forms of creative expression, we can tap into our inner world, express our unique perspectives, and connect with others on a deeper level. Creativity can be a source of joy, inspiration, and personal growth.

But what about material possessions and financial security? While they are not the sole determinants of the good life, they can certainly contribute to our well-being. Having our basic needs met, such as food, shelter, and healthcare, is essential for a good life. Financial security can provide us with peace of mind and the freedom to pursue our passions and goals.

However, it is important to remember that material possessions and financial wealth do not guarantee happiness or fulfillment. In fact, research has shown that beyond a certain level of income, additional wealth does not lead to significant increases in happiness. The pursuit of material possessions can even become a distraction from what truly matters in life.

Ultimately, the good life is a multifaceted concept that encompasses a wide range of factors, including happiness, meaning, purpose, relationships, personal growth, creativity, and social contribution.

There is no single definition of the good life that applies to everyone. What matters most is that we live our lives in accordance with our values, that we pursue our passions and goals, and that we strive to make a positive impact on the world.

As we continue to contemplate the good life, we must also be mindful of the challenges and obstacles that we face. Life is not always easy, and we will inevitably encounter setbacks, disappointments, and even tragedies. But even in the face of adversity, we can find meaning and purpose. We can learn from our experiences, grow as individuals, and find new ways to thrive.

Ultimately, the good life is not a destination, but a journey. It is a journey of self-discovery, growth, and contribution. By embracing this journey, we can create a life that is rich, meaningful, and fulfilling.

𝇋𝇋𝇋

The good life is not a destination, but a journey of continuous growth, learning, and contribution. It is a life lived with intention, purpose, and a deep appreciation for the beauty and complexity of the world around us. Seek happiness, cultivate meaningful relationships, and pursue your passions with unwavering determination.

SIX

DOES GOD EXIST? WRESTLING WITH FAITH AND REASON.

Does God exist? This question has been a source of contemplation, debate, and even conflict throughout human history. It is a question that transcends cultural boundaries, philosophical traditions, and religious beliefs. It is a question that touches upon our deepest fears, hopes, and aspirations. As we grapple with this question, we find ourselves wrestling with the complex relationship between faith and reason, two powerful forces that shape our understanding of the world and our place in it.

Faith, in its broadest sense, is a belief in something that cannot be proven or disproven by empirical evidence. It is a trust in something beyond our senses, a conviction that there is more to reality than what we can see and touch. For many, faith is a source of comfort, guidance, and meaning in life. It can provide a framework for understanding our existence, a moral compass to guide our actions, and a hope for a better future.

Reason, on the other hand, is the faculty of the mind that allows us to think logically, to analyze evidence, and to draw conclusions based on sound reasoning. It is the tool we use to understand the natural world, to solve problems, and to make informed decisions. Reason is often seen as the antithesis of faith, as it relies on empirical evidence and logical deduction rather than belief in the unseen.

The relationship between faith and reason has been a subject of debate for centuries. Some argue that faith and reason are incompatible, that one must choose between believing in something without evidence and relying on rational inquiry. Others argue that faith and reason can coexist, that they are complementary ways of knowing that can enrich and inform each other.

Theologians and philosophers have offered a variety of arguments for the existence of God, some based on faith and others based on reason. The ontological argument, for example, is a purely logical argument that attempts to prove the existence of God from the very concept of God. The cosmological argument, on the other hand, is based on the observation that the universe exists and must have a cause, which is ultimately God. The teleological argument, also known as the argument from design, argues that the complexity and order of the universe suggest the existence of an intelligent designer.

These arguments have been debated and criticized for centuries, and there is no consensus among philosophers or theologians about their validity. Some find them compelling, while others find them flawed or unconvincing. Ultimately, the question of whether or not God exists is a matter of personal belief, and each individual must decide for themselves what they believe and why.

For many, faith is not simply a matter of intellectual assent to a set of propositions, but a lived experience that shapes their entire worldview. It is a relationship with the divine, a sense of awe and wonder at the mysteries of the universe, a feeling of gratitude for the gift of life. Faith can inspire acts of great kindness, compassion, and selflessness, but it can also lead to intolerance, bigotry, and even violence.

Reason, too, can be a powerful force for good or ill. It can lead to scientific discoveries that improve our lives, to social reforms that promote justice and equality, and to philosophical insights that deepen our understanding of ourselves and the world around us. But reason can also be used to justify selfishness, cruelty, and oppression.

The challenge, then, is to find a way to integrate faith and reason, to use both to guide our lives and to shape our understanding of the world. This requires humility, open-mindedness, and a willingness to engage in respectful dialogue with those who hold different beliefs. It also requires a recognition that there are limits to both faith and reason, that there are some things that we may never fully understand.

Ultimately, the question of whether or not God exists is not simply a matter of intellectual curiosity. It is a question that has profound implications for our lives, our relationships, and our place in the world. It is a question that challenges us to think deeply about our values, our beliefs, and our ultimate purpose.

As we wrestle with this question, we must be mindful of the power of both faith and reason. We must seek to understand the perspectives of those who hold different beliefs, and we must be willing to question our own assumptions and biases. By engaging in this process of dialogue and inquiry, we can deepen our understanding of ourselves, of the world around us, and of the ultimate mystery of existence.

ppp

The question of God's existence has perplexed humanity for centuries. It is a question that transcends reason and logic, touching upon our deepest fears, hopes, and aspirations. Whether through faith or reason, seek to understand your own beliefs and find meaning in the mysteries of the universe.

SEVEN

WHAT HAPPENS WHEN WE DIE? PONDERING MORTALITY AND THE AFTERLIFE.

What happens when we die? This is perhaps the most profound and enigmatic question that humanity has ever contemplated. It is a question that has haunted our minds, inspired our art and literature, and shaped our religious and philosophical beliefs. The contemplation of mortality and the afterlife is a journey that takes us to the very heart of the human condition, forcing us to confront our deepest fears, hopes, and uncertainties.

Death is an inevitable part of life, a universal experience that touches every living being. Yet, despite its ubiquity, death remains a mystery, a final frontier that we cannot cross. The cessation of life, the end of consciousness, the disintegration of the body – these are concepts that are both terrifying and fascinating. They raise profound questions about the nature of our existence, the meaning of life, and the possibility of an afterlife.

Throughout history, different cultures and religions have offered diverse perspectives on what happens after death. Some believe in reincarnation, the idea that the soul is reborn into a new body after death, while others believe in heaven and hell, eternal realms of reward and punishment. Some envision an ancestral spirit world where the departed continue to interact with the living, while others simply believe that death is the end of everything.

The concept of the afterlife is deeply rooted in our human desire for continuity and transcendence. We long to believe that our lives have meaning and purpose beyond our earthly existence. We want to believe that our loved ones who have passed away are still with us in some way, that they continue to exist in another realm. The belief in an afterlife can provide comfort and solace in the face of death, offering hope for a reunion with loved ones and a continuation of our journey.

However, the question of the afterlife is not simply a matter of faith or belief. It is also a question of reason and evidence. Can we find any scientific or philosophical basis for believing in an afterlife? Many have argued that there is no empirical evidence to support the existence of an afterlife, that consciousness ceases to exist with the death of the brain, and that the idea of a soul is simply a comforting illusion.

Others point to near-death experiences, reports of out-of-body experiences, and other anecdotal evidence as suggesting that consciousness may indeed survive death. However, these experiences are often difficult to interpret and can be explained by natural phenomena. For example, near-death experiences may be caused by changes in brain chemistry or oxygen deprivation, rather than a glimpse of the afterlife.

The question of the afterlife is not only a matter of personal belief, but also a matter of cultural and social significance. Religious beliefs about the afterlife have played a crucial role in shaping human societies, influencing everything from funeral rites and burial practices to moral codes and social hierarchies. They have provided a framework for understanding death, a way to cope with grief and loss, and a hope for a better future.

The contemplation of mortality can also have a profound impact on our lives, even if we do not believe in an afterlife. It can inspire us to live more fully, to cherish each moment, and to make the most of our time on earth. It can motivate us to pursue our dreams, to connect with others, and to leave a positive legacy.

The awareness of our mortality can also lead us to question the meaning and purpose of our lives. Why are we here? What is the point of it all? If death is the end, does life have any inherent value? These are difficult questions, but they are also important ones. They force us to confront our own values and priorities, to think deeply about what truly matters to us.

Some find meaning in the pursuit of pleasure and happiness, while others find it in service to others, in creative expression, or in the pursuit of knowledge and understanding. Still, others find meaning in simply being present in the moment, appreciating the beauty of the world around them, and cherishing the relationships they have with others.

The contemplation of mortality and the afterlife is a journey that takes us to the very heart of the human condition. It is a journey that challenges us to confront our deepest fears, hopes, and uncertainties. It is a journey that can lead us to a deeper appreciation for life, a greater sense of purpose, and a more profound connection to the world around us.

As we ponder this question, we must be open to different perspectives, willing to question our own assumptions, and respectful of the beliefs of others. We must seek to understand the complexities of death and the afterlife, while also acknowledging the limits of our knowledge and understanding.

Ultimately, the question of what happens when we die may remain a mystery. But the very act of pondering this question can enrich our lives, deepen our understanding of ourselves and the world around us, and help us to live more fully and meaningfully. Whether or not we believe in an afterlife, the contemplation of mortality can remind us to cherish the time we have, to embrace the present moment, and to make the most of our precious lives.

ϸϸϸ

Death is an inevitable part of life, a mystery that has captivated and terrified us since time immemorial. While we may not know what lies beyond, we can choose to live each day to the fullest, cherishing our loved ones, pursuing our dreams, and leaving a positive legacy.

EIGHT

WHAT IS LOVE? UNPACKING THE COMPLEXITIES OF EMOTION.

What is love? It's a question that has echoed through the ages, whispered in poetry, sung in ballads, and pondered by philosophers. It's a question that resonates deeply within each of us, for love is a fundamental human experience, a force that shapes our lives, relationships, and understanding of the world. Yet, despite its universality, love remains an elusive and complex emotion, defying easy definition and categorization. In this exploration, we will delve into the multifaceted nature of love, unpacking its various forms, expressions, and the profound impact it has on our lives.

At its core, love is a deep feeling of affection and care for another being. It is a force that draws us towards others, fostering connection, intimacy, and a sense of belonging. Love can be expressed in a myriad of ways, from the passionate embrace of romantic partners to the unwavering support of family and friends, to the tender care we offer to pets and even the reverence we feel for nature or a higher power.

Romantic love, often celebrated in art and literature, is perhaps the most recognizable and idealized form of love. It is a passionate and intense emotion, characterized by feelings of attraction, desire, and longing. Romantic love can be all-consuming, making us feel alive and exhilarated, as if we are on top of the world. It can inspire acts of great kindness, sacrifice, and devotion.

Yet, romantic love is not without its complexities. It can be fueled by infatuation, idealized projections, and unrealistic expectations. It can be fickle, waxing and waning with the ebb and flow of emotions. It can be possessive, jealous, and even destructive. The challenges of romantic love lie in balancing passion with reason, maintaining intimacy over time, and navigating the inevitable conflicts that arise in any relationship.

Beyond romantic love, there are countless other forms of love that enrich our lives. Familial love, the bond we share with our parents, siblings, and children, is a love that is often unconditional, unwavering, and deeply rooted in shared history and experiences. It is a love that nurtures us, protects us, and provides a foundation for our personal growth and development.

Platonic love, the love between friends, is a love that is based on mutual respect, trust, and understanding. It is a love that celebrates individuality, supports personal growth, and provides a safe space for vulnerability and authenticity. Platonic love can be just as fulfilling and meaningful as romantic love, offering companionship, laughter, and shared experiences.

Love is not limited to human relationships. We can also feel love for animals, nature, art, music, and even ideas. This type of love can be just as powerful and transformative as the love we feel for other people. It can inspire us to care for the environment, appreciate beauty, pursue knowledge, and make a positive impact on the world.

The complexities of love lie not only in its various forms but also in the way it is expressed. Love can be expressed through words, actions, touch, and even silence. It can be expressed through grand gestures or small acts of kindness. It can be expressed through laughter, tears, or simply a knowing glance.

The expression of love is often shaped by cultural norms and individual preferences. Some cultures are more expressive than others, while some individuals are more comfortable expressing love through actions rather than words. Regardless of how it is expressed, love is a powerful force that can transcend cultural boundaries and individual differences.

Love is not always easy. It requires vulnerability, trust, and a willingness to open ourselves up to the possibility of pain and disappointment. It requires us to be patient, forgiving, and understanding. It requires us to communicate openly and honestly, to listen with empathy, and to compromise when necessary.

But the rewards of love are immeasurable. Love can bring us joy, happiness, and a sense of purpose. It can heal our wounds, inspire us to be better versions of ourselves, and give us the courage to face life's challenges. Love can connect us to others in a way that transcends the boundaries of self, creating a sense of belonging and community.

The journey of love is a lifelong one. It is a journey that takes us through the highs and lows of human experience, from the ecstasy of new love to the depths of heartbreak and loss. It is a journey that challenges us to grow, to learn, and to become more compassionate, understanding, and loving human beings.

Ultimately, love is a mystery, a force that we may never fully comprehend. But it is a mystery worth exploring, for it is through love that we truly come alive. It is through love that we find meaning, purpose, and connection in this vast and ever-changing world.

ﬗﬗﬗ

Love is a complex and multifaceted emotion that encompasses passion, intimacy, loyalty, friendship, and compassion. It is a force that can lift us to great heights of joy and plunge us into the depths of despair. Embrace love in all its forms, nurture your relationships, and let it be a guiding light in your life.

NINE

WHAT IS BEAUTY? APPRECIATING ART AND AESTHETICS.

What is beauty? This deceptively simple question has been pondered by philosophers, artists, poets, and thinkers throughout history. It is a question that transcends cultures and epochs, yet remains deeply personal and subjective. The quest to define beauty takes us on a journey through the realms of art, aesthetics, and the very nature of human perception and appreciation.

At its core, beauty is a quality that evokes a sense of pleasure, awe, or admiration in the observer. It is a subjective experience, shaped by individual preferences, cultural backgrounds, and personal experiences. What one person finds beautiful, another may not, and what was considered beautiful in one era may be seen as mundane or even ugly in another. This inherent subjectivity makes defining beauty a challenging task.

Philosophers have long debated the nature of beauty, with some arguing that it is an objective quality inherent in the object itself, while others believe that it is entirely dependent on the observer's perception. Plato, for example, believed that beauty was an ideal form that existed in a realm beyond the physical world, and that objects in the physical world were beautiful only to the extent that they participated in this ideal form.

Others, like David Hume, argued that beauty is a subjective experience, a feeling of pleasure or satisfaction that arises in the observer's mind. There is no objective standard of beauty, and what we find beautiful is simply a matter of personal taste.

Despite the lack of a universally agreed-upon definition, there are certain qualities that are often associated with beauty. These include symmetry, harmony, balance, proportion, and complexity. These qualities can be found in a wide range of objects, from natural landscapes to works of art to human faces.

Art plays a crucial role in our understanding and appreciation of beauty. Artists throughout history have sought to capture and express beauty in their creations, whether through painting, sculpture, music, literature, or other forms of artistic expression. Art can evoke a wide range of emotions, from joy and awe to sadness and contemplation. It can challenge our perceptions, expand our horizons, and enrich our lives in countless ways.

Aesthetics, the branch of philosophy concerned with the nature of art, beauty, and taste, provides a framework for understanding our aesthetic experiences. It explores questions such as: What makes a work of art beautiful? How do we judge aesthetic quality? What is the role of art in society? By examining these questions, aesthetics can help us to better understand our own aesthetic preferences and to appreciate the beauty that surrounds us.

The appreciation of beauty is not just a matter of personal taste, but also a matter of cultural and historical context. Different cultures have different aesthetic traditions, and what is considered beautiful in one culture may not be in another. For example, the ideal of feminine beauty in Western art has changed dramatically over time, from the voluptuous figures of the Renaissance to the slender silhouettes of the modern era.

Our appreciation of beauty is also influenced by our personal experiences and values. We may find beauty in objects or experiences that resonate with our own emotions, memories, or beliefs. A piece of music may evoke a sense of nostalgia, a painting may remind us of a loved one, or a natural landscape may fill us with a sense of peace and tranquility.

The experience of beauty is not just a passive one. It can also be an active and engaging process. When we encounter something beautiful, we often want to explore it further, to understand its complexities and nuances. We may want to share our experience with others, to discuss and debate its merits. This active engagement with beauty can deepen our appreciation and enrich our lives.

In a world that is often chaotic and stressful, the appreciation of beauty can be a source of solace and inspiration. It can remind us of the inherent goodness and beauty of the world, and it can give us hope and joy in the face of adversity. Whether we find beauty in a sunset, a symphony, or a simple act of kindness, the experience of beauty can uplift our spirits, expand our minds, and connect us to something larger than ourselves.

The quest to define beauty is an ongoing one, and there may never be a single, definitive answer. But the journey itself is rewarding, leading us to a deeper understanding of ourselves, our world, and the power of art and aesthetics to enrich our lives.

ppp

Beauty is a subjective experience, a kaleidoscope of colors, sounds, and forms that ignite our senses and stir our souls. It is found in nature's grandeur, in the masterpieces of art, and in the everyday moments of life. Seek beauty, cultivate your aesthetic sensibilities, and let it enrich your life.

TEN

WHAT IS TIME? UNRAVELING THE MYSTERIES OF PAST, PRESENT, AND FUTURE.

What is time? This seemingly simple question has perplexed philosophers, scientists, and thinkers for millennia. It is a fundamental concept that permeates our lives, shaping our experiences, our understanding of the world, and our very sense of self. Yet, despite its ubiquity, time remains an elusive and enigmatic concept, defying easy definition and comprehension. In this exploration, we will delve into the mysteries of time, unraveling its nature, its relationship to the past, present, and future, and its profound impact on our lives.

Time is often described as a linear progression, a continuous flow from the past through the present and into the future. We measure time in seconds, minutes, hours, days, years, and centuries. We mark its passage with clocks, calendars, and anniversaries. We use time to organize our lives, to plan for the future, and to reflect on the past.

But is time truly linear? Or is it a more complex and multidimensional phenomenon? Some physicists and philosophers have proposed that time may be an illusion, a construct of our minds that helps us make sense of the world around us. Others have suggested that time may be cyclical, repeating itself in an endless loop. Still, others have proposed that time may be a dimension, like space, that we can move through in different directions.

Einstein's theory of relativity revolutionized our understanding of time, showing that it is not absolute but relative to the observer. Time can slow down or speed up depending on the observer's motion and the strength of the gravitational field they are in. This means that there is no single, universal time, but rather a multitude of times, each relative to a particular frame of reference.

The concept of the past, present, and future is also intertwined with our understanding of time. The past is the realm of memory and history, where we store our experiences and knowledge. The present is the fleeting moment of now, where we experience the world directly. The future is the realm of anticipation and possibility, where we imagine what may come to be.

But what is the nature of the past, present, and future? Are they fixed and unchanging, or are they malleable and subject to interpretation? Some philosophers argue that the past is immutable, that what has happened cannot be undone. Others suggest that the past is constantly being reinterpreted and re-evaluated in light of new experiences and information.

The present, too, is a complex and elusive concept. It is the moment of now, yet it is constantly slipping away into the past. The present is the only time we can truly experience the world, yet it is also the most difficult time to grasp. We are constantly bombarded with sensory input, thoughts, and emotions, making it difficult to focus on the present moment.

The future is perhaps the most mysterious of all. It is the realm of the unknown, the yet-to-be. We can imagine the future, we can plan for it, but we cannot know for certain what it holds. The future is full of possibilities, both good and bad. It is a source of both hope and anxiety.

Time plays a crucial role in our lives. It shapes our experiences, our memories, and our sense of self. We are constantly changing beings, evolving and transforming over time. Our bodies age, our minds develop, and our relationships evolve. Time is the medium through which we experience this change, the canvas upon which we paint the story of our lives.

Our perception of time also changes as we age. Children often experience time as slow and expansive, with endless days stretching out before them. Adults, on the other hand, often feel that time is speeding up, that the years are slipping away faster and faster. This may be due to the fact that as we get older, we have more experiences and memories to compare the present moment to, making it seem shorter in comparison.

Time is also a source of anxiety and stress. We worry about not having enough time, about deadlines, about aging, and about death. We feel pressure to achieve our goals, to make the most of our time, and to leave a lasting legacy. This pressure can lead to burnout, anxiety, and even depression.

But time can also be a source of joy and wonder. We can experience timelessness in moments of deep connection with others, in the beauty of nature, or in the creative flow of artistic expression. We can find meaning and purpose in the passage of time, as we witness the growth and development of our loved ones, contribute to our communities, and leave a positive impact on the world.

In the end, the mystery of time remains. It is a concept that we may never fully understand, but it is one that we cannot ignore. Time is a fundamental part of our existence, shaping our experiences, our relationships, and our understanding of the world. By exploring the mysteries of time, we can gain a deeper appreciation for the preciousness of life, the importance of living in the present moment, and the power of time to shape our destiny.

ᐅᐅᐅ

Time is a relentless river, carrying us forward on its currents. It is a measure of our experiences, a marker of our milestones, and a reminder of our mortality. Embrace the present moment, cherish the memories of the past, and look towards the future with hope and anticipation.

ELEVEN

WHAT IS KNOWLEDGE? UNDERSTANDING HOW WE LEARN AND KNOW.

What is knowledge? This seemingly simple question has been a central concern of philosophers, scientists, and thinkers for centuries. It is a question that delves into the very core of human cognition, exploring how we acquire, process, and utilize information to understand the world around us. Knowledge is not merely a collection of facts or data; it is a complex and multifaceted phenomenon that encompasses our beliefs, experiences, and understanding of the world. In this exploration, we will delve into the nature of knowledge, examining how we learn and know, the different types of knowledge, and the challenges and limitations we face in our pursuit of understanding.

At its most basic level, knowledge can be defined as justified true belief. This means that for something to be considered knowledge, it must be true, we must believe it to be true, and our belief must be justified by evidence or reason. However, this definition is not without its complexities and controversies. Philosophers have debated the nature of truth, the role of belief, and the criteria for justification.

One of the most fundamental questions about knowledge is how we acquire it. Empiricism, a philosophical school of thought, emphasizes the role of sensory experience in the acquisition of knowledge. According to empiricists, we gain knowledge through observation, experimentation, and interaction with the world around us. Our senses provide us with raw data, which our minds then process and interpret to form beliefs about the world.

Another philosophical school of thought, rationalism, emphasizes the role of reason and innate ideas in the acquisition of knowledge. Rationalists argue that some knowledge is not derived from experience but is inherent in our minds. These innate ideas, such as the concept of numbers or the laws of logic, provide a foundation for our understanding of the world.

In reality, most of our knowledge is acquired through a combination of both empirical and rational processes. We learn through observation and experience, but we also use reason and logic to interpret and organize that information. We form hypotheses, test them through experimentation, and revise our beliefs based on the evidence.

Knowledge can be classified into different types, each with its own characteristics and methods of acquisition. Propositional knowledge, or knowledge-that, refers to our knowledge of facts or truths. For example, we know that the Earth is round, that water boils at 100 degrees Celsius, or that Paris is the capital of France. This type of knowledge is often acquired through education, reading, or direct experience.

Procedural knowledge, or knowledge-how, refers to our knowledge of how to do things. This includes skills such as riding a bicycle, playing a musical instrument, or speaking a foreign language. Procedural knowledge is typically acquired through practice and experience.

Personal knowledge, or knowledge by acquaintance, refers to our knowledge of people, places, or things through direct experience. For example, we know our friends and family members, the city we live in, or our favorite foods. This type of knowledge is gained through direct interaction and engagement with the world.

The pursuit of knowledge is not without its challenges. One of the most significant challenges is the problem of skepticism. Skeptics argue that we can never be certain of anything, that our senses can deceive us, and that our reasoning can be flawed. They question whether we can ever truly know anything with absolute certainty.

Another challenge is the vastness and complexity of the world. There is simply too much information for any one person to know everything. We must rely on experts, trust reliable sources of information, and constantly update our knowledge as new discoveries are made.

Furthermore, the rapid pace of technological change and the proliferation of information in the digital age have created new challenges for knowledge acquisition and evaluation. We are constantly bombarded with information from a variety of sources, some reliable and some not. It is important to develop critical thinking skills to evaluate the information we encounter and to discern truth from falsehood.

Despite these challenges, the pursuit of knowledge is a fundamental human endeavor. It is through knowledge that we understand the world, make informed decisions, and solve problems. Knowledge empowers us to improve our lives, to create new technologies, and to build a better future.

The quest for knowledge is not just a matter of accumulating facts and information. It is also about understanding the relationships between those facts, the underlying principles that govern the world, and the implications of our knowledge for our lives and society. It is a lifelong journey of exploration, discovery, and growth.

As we continue our journey of understanding how we learn and know, we must be mindful of the challenges and limitations we face. We must be open to new ideas, willing to question our assumptions, and always strive for a deeper understanding of the world around us. For it is through knowledge that we unlock our full potential as human beings and create a brighter future for ourselves and for generations to come

ϷϷϷ

Freedom is a precious gift, a birthright that allows us to chart our own course in life. It is the power to choose, to act, and to express ourselves authentically. Embrace your freedom, but remember that it comes with responsibility.

TWELVE

WHAT IS FREEDOM? GRAPPLING WITH CHOICES AND CONSEQUENCES.

What is freedom? This question has been a driving force behind countless revolutions, philosophical debates, and personal quests for self-determination. It is a concept that ignites our imaginations, fuels our aspirations, and challenges us to confront the complexities of choice and consequence. Freedom is not merely the absence of constraints, but a dynamic and multifaceted concept that encompasses individual autonomy, social responsibility, and the pursuit of a meaningful life. In this exploration, we will delve into the nature of freedom, examining its various dimensions, the choices it presents, and the consequences that follow.

At its core, freedom can be defined as the ability to act, speak, or think as one wants without hindrance or restraint. It is the power to make choices, to pursue our goals, and to live our lives according to our own values and beliefs. Freedom is often seen as a fundamental human right, essential for our well-being and flourishing.

However, freedom is not absolute. It is limited by various factors, including physical constraints, social norms, and the rights and freedoms of others. We cannot fly like birds, violate the laws of physics, or harm others without facing consequences. Our freedom is always constrained by the realities of the world we live in.

One of the most important aspects of freedom is the ability to make choices. We are constantly faced with choices, both big and small, that shape the course of our lives. Some choices are trivial, such as what to wear or what to eat for breakfast. Others are more significant, such as choosing a career path, a life partner, or a moral stance on a particular issue.

The ability to make choices is often seen as a hallmark of freedom, but it is not without its challenges. Choices can be difficult, especially when they involve competing values, uncertain outcomes, or significant risks. The fear of making the wrong choice can lead to indecision, anxiety, and even paralysis.

The choices we make have consequences, both for ourselves and for others. Some consequences are immediate and obvious, while others may be delayed or unforeseen. Our choices can shape our relationships, our careers, our health, and our overall well-being. They can also impact the lives of others, for better or for worse.

The concept of responsibility is closely linked to freedom. With the freedom to make choices comes the responsibility to bear the consequences of those choices. We are accountable for our actions, and we must be willing to accept the consequences, whether they are positive or negative.

The relationship between freedom and responsibility is complex and often contentious. Some argue that individuals should be held fully responsible for their choices, regardless of their circumstances or background. Others believe that societal factors, such as poverty, discrimination, or lack of opportunity, can limit individual freedom and mitigate personal responsibility.

The question of how much freedom individuals should have and how much responsibility they should bear is a matter of ongoing debate. Different societies and cultures have different answers to this question, and there is no easy or universally agreed-upon solution.

In addition to individual freedom, there is also the concept of social freedom. This refers to the freedom of a society or community to govern itself, to determine its own values and priorities, and to pursue its own collective goals. Social freedom is often seen as essential for the flourishing of a society, allowing it to adapt to changing circumstances and to meet the needs of its members.

However, social freedom can also conflict with individual freedom. For example, a society may impose restrictions on individual behavior in order to promote the common good, such as laws against theft or violence. The balance between individual and social freedom is a delicate one, and it is constantly evolving as societies change and new challenges arise.

The pursuit of freedom is not just an individual endeavor; it is also a collective one. We can work together to create a society that values and protects individual freedoms while also promoting social justice and equality. We can advocate for policies that empower individuals, expand opportunities, and address systemic inequalities.

Freedom is not a static state, but a dynamic process. It is a journey of self-discovery, growth, and responsibility. By embracing our freedom, making informed choices, and accepting the consequences of our actions, we can create a life that is meaningful, fulfilling, and truly our own.

❦❦❦

Justice is the cornerstone of a fair and equitable society. It is the principle that ensures everyone is treated with dignity, respect, and equality. Seek justice, challenge injustice, and strive to create a world where everyone has the opportunity to thrive.

THIRTEEN

WHAT IS JUSTICE? EXAMINING FAIRNESS AND EQUALITY.

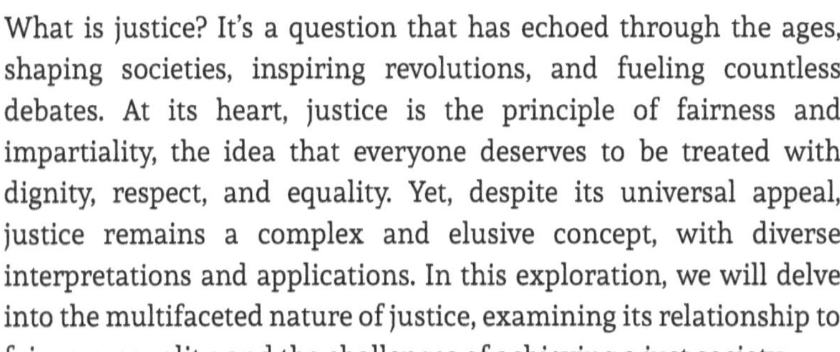

What is justice? It's a question that has echoed through the ages, shaping societies, inspiring revolutions, and fueling countless debates. At its heart, justice is the principle of fairness and impartiality, the idea that everyone deserves to be treated with dignity, respect, and equality. Yet, despite its universal appeal, justice remains a complex and elusive concept, with diverse interpretations and applications. In this exploration, we will delve into the multifaceted nature of justice, examining its relationship to fairness, equality, and the challenges of achieving a just society.

Fairness is a fundamental principle of justice. It is the idea that everyone should be treated equally, regardless of their race, gender, religion, or socioeconomic status. Fairness requires that we consider the needs and interests of all individuals, not just the privileged or powerful. It demands that we make decisions based on objective criteria, rather than personal biases or prejudices.

Equality is another crucial aspect of justice. It is the principle that everyone should have the same opportunities and access to resources, regardless of their background or circumstances. Equality ensures that everyone has a fair chance to succeed in life, to pursue their dreams, and to reach their full potential.

However, fairness and equality are not always easy to achieve. In many societies, there are systemic inequalities that disadvantage certain groups of people. These inequalities can be based on race, gender, class, or other factors. They can manifest in unequal access to education, healthcare, employment, and other essential resources.

Achieving justice requires addressing these systemic inequalities and creating a society where everyone has a fair chance to succeed. This may involve implementing policies that promote equal opportunity, such as affirmative action programs or progressive taxation. It may also involve challenging discriminatory practices and attitudes, and working to create a more inclusive and equitable society.

Justice is not just about treating everyone equally, but also about recognizing and addressing the unique needs and vulnerabilities of different individuals and groups. For example, children and the elderly may require special protections, while people with disabilities may need additional support to fully participate in society.

Justice is also about holding individuals and institutions accountable for their actions. When someone breaks the law or harms another person, justice demands that they be held responsible for their actions. This may involve punishment, such as fines or imprisonment, but it can also involve restorative justice practices that seek to repair the harm done and reconcile the offender with the victim and the community.

The pursuit of justice is not just a matter of legal or political systems, but also a matter of personal ethics and morality. We can all contribute to a more just society by treating others with fairness and respect, by speaking out against injustice, and by working to create a more equitable and inclusive world.

The concept of justice is not static, but evolves over time in response to changing social, cultural, and economic conditions. What was considered just in one era may be seen as unjust in another. For example, slavery was once considered legal and even morally justifiable, but today it is universally condemned as a grave injustice.

The challenges of achieving justice are many and complex. They require us to confront difficult questions about power, privilege, and the distribution of resources. They require us to grapple with conflicting values and priorities, and to find ways to balance individual rights with the needs of the community.

But the pursuit of justice is also a noble and inspiring endeavor. It is a pursuit that speaks to our deepest values and aspirations, our longing for a world where everyone is treated with dignity, respect, and equality. By striving for justice, we not only create a better world for ourselves and others, but we also fulfill our own potential as human beings.

ppp

Society is a tapestry woven with threads of diverse cultures, beliefs, and values. It is a dynamic and ever-evolving entity that shapes our identities, relationships, and aspirations. Embrace diversity, seek understanding, and contribute to the betterment of your community.

FOURTEEN

WHAT IS SOCIETY? REFLECTING ON COMMUNITIES AND CULTURES.

What is society? This seemingly straightforward question opens up a vast and complex landscape of human interaction, shared values, and cultural diversity. Society is more than just a collection of individuals; it is a dynamic and intricate web of relationships, institutions, and shared beliefs that shape our lives and identities.

In this exploration, we will delve into the nature of society, reflecting on the roles of communities, cultures, and the intricate dance between individual and collective identities.

At its core, society is a group of people living together in a more or less ordered community. It is a system of interconnected individuals who share a common culture, values, and institutions. Societies can be small and intimate, like a close-knit village, or vast and complex, like a sprawling metropolis.

They can be homogeneous, with shared cultural and linguistic backgrounds, or diverse, encompassing a wide range of ethnicities, religions, and lifestyles.

Communities are the building blocks of society. They are groups of people who share a common identity, whether based on geography, ethnicity, religion, shared interests, or other factors. Communities provide a sense of belonging, support, and shared purpose.

They offer a space for individuals to connect with others, to build relationships, and to contribute to the collective good.

Communities can be found at various levels, from local neighborhoods to national or even global communities. They can be formal, with clearly defined structures and roles, or informal, based on shared interests or social networks.

Communities play a crucial role in shaping our identities, values, and beliefs. They provide us with a sense of place, a sense of history, and a sense of belonging.

Culture is the glue that binds a society together. It is the shared values, beliefs, customs, behaviors, and artifacts that characterize a group of people. Culture encompasses everything from language and religion to art, music, and cuisine.

It is transmitted from one generation to the next through socialization, education, and shared experiences.

Culture provides a framework for understanding the world and our place in it. It shapes our values, our beliefs, and our behaviors. It influences how we interact with others, how we express ourselves, and how we make sense of our experiences. Culture is not static; it is constantly evolving and adapting in response to new challenges and opportunities.

The relationship between individual and society is a complex and dynamic one. We are both shaped by and shape the society in which we live. Our individual choices and actions can contribute to social change, while societal norms and institutions can influence our individual behavior and beliefs.

The tension between individual freedom and social responsibility is a perennial theme in social and political philosophy. We value individual autonomy and the right to pursue our own goals and interests. Yet, we also recognize that we have a responsibility to contribute to the well-being of our communities and to uphold the values and norms that bind us together.

The challenge of creating a just and equitable society is one that has occupied philosophers and social reformers for centuries. How do we balance individual rights with the needs of the community?

How do we ensure that everyone has a fair chance to succeed, regardless of their background or circumstances? How do we create a society that is both diverse and cohesive, where individuals from different backgrounds can live together in harmony?

These are complex questions with no easy answers. But by reflecting on the nature of society, communities, and cultures, we can gain a deeper understanding of the challenges and opportunities we face. We can learn to appreciate the diversity of human experience, while also recognizing the common values and aspirations that unite us.

In a world that is becoming increasingly interconnected, the concept of society is expanding beyond national borders.

We are witnessing the emergence of global communities, united by shared values, interests, and concerns. The challenges we face, such as climate change, poverty, and inequality, are global in scope and require global solutions.

As we navigate this complex and ever-changing world, it is important to remember that we are all part of something larger than ourselves.

We are members of communities, citizens of nations, and ultimately, members of the global human family. By working together, we can create a society that is more just, equitable, and sustainable for all.

ᗡᗡᗡ

Nature is a symphony of interconnected systems, a breathtaking display of beauty and complexity. It is the source of our sustenance, our inspiration, and our connection to the living world. Cherish nature, protect its fragile ecosystems, and live in harmony with the environment.

FIFTEEN

WHAT IS NATURE? CONTEMPLATING THE ENVIRONMENT AND OUR PLACE IN IT.

What is nature? This seemingly simple question opens up a vast and complex universe of interconnected systems, awe-inspiring beauty, and profound ecological significance. It invites us to contemplate not only the physical world around us – the mountains, rivers, forests, and oceans – but also our own place within this intricate web of life. As we embark on this contemplation, we delve into the essence of nature, exploring its diverse manifestations, its intrinsic value, and the intricate relationship between humans and the environment.

Nature, in its broadest sense, encompasses everything that exists in the physical world independent of human creation. It is the totality of the living and non-living components of the Earth, including plants, animals, microorganisms, rocks, soil, water, and the atmosphere. Nature is a dynamic and ever-changing system, shaped by intricate interactions between its various components, driven by the forces of evolution, climate, and geological processes.

The natural world is a source of immense beauty and wonder. From the majestic grandeur of snow-capped mountains to the vibrant colors of a coral reef, from the intricate patterns of a butterfly's wings to the vastness of the starry sky, nature offers a limitless array of aesthetic experiences that inspire awe and reverence. It is a source of artistic inspiration, spiritual renewal, and emotional well-being.

But nature is not just about beauty; it is also a complex and interconnected system that provides essential ecosystem services upon which human life and well-being depend. These services include the provision of clean air and water, the regulation of climate, the pollination of crops, the decomposition of waste, and the maintenance of biodiversity. Nature provides us with food, fuel, medicine, and other resources essential for our survival and prosperity.

The relationship between humans and nature is a complex and dynamic one. We are both a part of nature and a force that shapes it. Our actions have profound impacts on the environment, both positive and negative. We have the power to protect and restore nature, but we also have the power to degrade and destroy it.

Throughout history, humans have relied on nature for sustenance and survival. We have harvested its resources, cultivated its lands, and built civilizations in its midst. But as our population has grown and our technological capabilities have expanded, our impact on the environment has become increasingly significant.

Human activities, such as deforestation, pollution, and climate change, are causing widespread environmental degradation and loss of biodiversity. We are altering the Earth's ecosystems at an unprecedented rate, pushing many species to the brink of extinction and threatening the delicate balance of the planet's natural systems.

The consequences of our actions are becoming increasingly evident. We are experiencing more frequent and intense natural disasters, such as floods, droughts, wildfires, and hurricanes. We are facing the threat of rising sea levels, which could displace millions of people and inundate coastal cities. We are witnessing the decline of pollinators, which are essential for food production. We are experiencing the spread of zoonotic diseases, which are transmitted from animals to humans.

The challenges we face are daunting, but they are not insurmountable. By recognizing our interconnectedness with nature and taking responsibility for our actions, we can begin to heal the wounds we have inflicted on the planet. We can adopt sustainable practices that minimize our environmental impact, protect endangered species, restore degraded ecosystems, and transition to clean and renewable sources of energy.

Education plays a crucial role in fostering environmental awareness and responsibility. By learning about the natural world, its complexities, and its vulnerabilities, we can develop a deeper appreciation for its value and a greater commitment to its protection. We can learn to live in harmony with nature, recognizing that our own well-being is inextricably linked to the health of the planet.

Ultimately, our relationship with nature is a reflection of our values and priorities. Do we see nature as a resource to be exploited, or as a sacred trust to be cherished and protected? Do we prioritize short-term economic gain over long-term environmental sustainability?

The choices we make today will determine the fate of our planet and the future of generations to come.

The contemplation of nature invites us to reflect on our place in the world, our responsibility to care for the environment, and the interconnectedness of all living beings. It is a journey of discovery, a journey that can lead to a deeper understanding of ourselves and our place in the cosmos.

As we continue to explore the mysteries of nature, we must remember that we are not separate from it, but an integral part of it. Our actions have consequences, and we have a responsibility to make choices that will protect and restore the natural world for future generations. By embracing our connection to nature, we can find meaning, purpose, and a sense of belonging in this vast and wondrous universe.

ᐯᐯᐯ

The universe is a vast and mysterious expanse, a canvas of stars, galaxies, and untold wonders. It is a testament to the power of creation and the enduring quest to understand our place in the cosmos. Explore the universe, marvel at its beauty, and ponder the mysteries that lie beyond.

SIXTEEN

WHAT IS THE UNIVERSE? PONDERING THE COSMOS AND ITS ORIGINS.

What is the universe? This question has captivated humanity for millennia, driving us to explore the vast expanse beyond our planet and ponder the mysteries of our cosmic origins. The universe, in its awe-inspiring grandeur, encompasses everything that exists – from the tiniest subatomic particles to the largest galaxies, from the energy that permeates space to the matter that forms stars and planets. It is a canvas of breathtaking beauty, a symphony of cosmic forces, and a testament to the profound interconnectedness of all things.

In our quest to understand the universe, we embark on a journey through time and space, tracing its evolution from the fiery crucible of the Big Bang to the present day. The prevailing scientific model, known as the Big Bang theory, suggests that the universe began as an infinitely hot and dense state some 13.8 billion years ago. In a cataclysmic explosion, space itself expanded and cooled, allowing matter and energy to coalesce into the stars, galaxies, and planets that we observe today.

The Big Bang theory is supported by a wealth of evidence, including the cosmic microwave background radiation, the afterglow of the Big Bang, and the observed redshift of distant galaxies, which indicates that the universe is expanding. However, the Big Bang theory does not explain everything. It does not tell us what existed before the Big Bang, nor does it explain the nature of dark matter and dark energy, two mysterious components that make up most of the universe's mass-energy content.

As we peer deeper into the cosmos, we encounter a breathtaking array of celestial objects and phenomena. Galaxies, vast collections of stars, gas, and dust, come in a variety of shapes and sizes, from majestic spirals to irregular dwarfs. Within these galaxies, stars are born, live, and die in spectacular fashion, forging the elements that make up our bodies and the world around us. Planets, once thought to be rare, are now known to be abundant, orbiting other stars in diverse configurations.

The universe is not a static entity but a dynamic and evolving one. Stars are born in the swirling clouds of gas and dust called nebulae, fueled by nuclear fusion that converts hydrogen into helium. As stars age, they evolve, changing in size, temperature, and luminosity. Massive stars end their lives in spectacular supernova explosions, scattering the elements they have created into space. These elements then become the building blocks for new stars, planets, and even life itself.

The universe is also home to a menagerie of exotic objects and phenomena. Black holes, regions of spacetime where gravity is so strong that nothing, not even light, can escape, are among the most mysterious and fascinating objects in the cosmos. Neutron stars, the remnants of massive stars that have collapsed under their own gravity, are incredibly dense and spin rapidly, emitting beams of radiation that sweep across the sky like cosmic lighthouses.

Dark matter and dark energy, while invisible to our telescopes, are thought to make up most of the universe's mass-energy content. Dark matter is a mysterious substance that does not interact with light, but its gravitational effects are evident in the motions of galaxies and clusters of galaxies. Dark energy, even more enigmatic, is a force that is causing the expansion of the universe to accelerate.

The study of the universe is not just about understanding its physical properties and constituents. It is also about exploring the profound questions that arise from our contemplation of the cosmos. What is our place in the universe? Are we alone, or is there other life out there? What is the ultimate fate of the universe?

These questions have been pondered by philosophers, theologians, and scientists for centuries. While we may never have definitive answers to all of them, the pursuit of knowledge and understanding is a fundamental part of the human experience. By exploring the cosmos, we not only gain a deeper appreciation for the beauty and complexity of the universe, but we also gain a better understanding of ourselves and our place in the grand scheme of things.

The universe is a source of wonder, inspiration, and humility. It is a reminder of our own smallness in the vast expanse of space and time, yet it also speaks to our potential for greatness. We are, after all, made of the same stuff as the stars, and we have the capacity to explore, to discover, and to understand the universe in ways that our ancestors could only dream of.

As we continue to explore the cosmos, we are constantly pushing the boundaries of our knowledge and understanding. We are developing new technologies that allow us to see farther into space and deeper into time. We are discovering new planets, new galaxies, and new phenomena that challenge our understanding of the universe.

The journey of cosmic exploration is far from over. There are still many mysteries to unravel, many questions to answer. But with each new discovery, we come closer to understanding the universe and our place within it. We are part of a grand cosmic story, a story that began billions of years ago and continues to unfold today.

ᐳᐳᐳ

Technology is a double-edged sword, a powerful tool that can be used for good or for ill. It has the potential to solve our most pressing challenges and enhance our lives in countless ways. Embrace technology, but use it wisely and ethically.

SEVENTEEN

HOW CAN WE CHANGE THE WORLD? CONSIDERING OUR ROLE IN SHAPING THE FUTURE.

How can we change the world? This question, brimming with both hope and trepidation, resonates deeply within each of us. We are born into a world filled with both beauty and injustice, opportunity and adversity, harmony and conflict. As we navigate this complex landscape, we yearn to make a positive impact, to leave our mark on the world, and to create a better future for ourselves and generations to come. But how can we, as individuals, truly make a difference? How can we shape the world in a way that aligns with our values and aspirations?

The notion of changing the world can seem daunting, even

overwhelming. The problems we face, from climate change to poverty to social injustice, can feel insurmountable. But it is precisely in these moments of challenge that we must remember the power of individual action. Every act of kindness, every voice raised for justice, every effort to make a positive impact, ripples outward, creating a wave of change that can transform our communities, our societies, and ultimately, our world.

One of the most powerful ways we can change the world is through our own personal choices and actions. The decisions we make every day, from what we eat and buy to how we consume energy and dispose of waste, have a ripple effect on the environment and society. By choosing to live sustainably, we can reduce our carbon footprint, conserve resources, and protect the planet for future generations. By choosing to support ethical businesses and social causes, we can contribute to a more just and equitable world.

But changing the world is not just about individual actions; it is also about collective action. We can join together with others who share our values and passions to advocate for change, to challenge injustice, and to build a better future. We can participate in community organizations, volunteer our time and talents, and use our voices to speak out against inequality and oppression.

Education plays a crucial role in shaping the future. By educating ourselves and others about the challenges facing our world, we can empower individuals to make informed choices, to advocate for change, and to develop innovative solutions. Education can also foster critical thinking, empathy, and a sense of global citizenship, which are essential for building a more just and sustainable world.

Innovation and technology have the potential to transform our world in profound ways. From renewable energy sources to medical breakthroughs to educational tools, technological advancements can improve our lives, address global challenges, and create new opportunities. However, it is important to ensure that technology is used ethically and responsibly, in ways that benefit all of humanity and the planet.

The arts and humanities also play a crucial role in shaping our world. They allow us to express ourselves, to connect with others, and to explore the complexities of the human experience. Through art, music, literature, and other forms of creative expression, we can challenge the status quo, inspire change, and imagine a better future.

The pursuit of social justice is another critical component of changing the world. We must work to dismantle systems of oppression and inequality, to ensure that everyone has equal access to opportunities and resources, and to create a society where all individuals are valued and respected. This may involve advocating for policy changes, participating in protests and demonstrations, or simply speaking out against injustice in our daily lives.

But perhaps the most important way we can change the world is by changing ourselves. By cultivating compassion, empathy, and understanding, we can break down barriers, build bridges, and foster a more inclusive and harmonious society. By developing our own inner strength, resilience, and wisdom, we can become agents of positive change in our communities and in the world.

Changing the world is not an easy task. It requires courage, perseverance, and a willingness to take risks. It requires us to step outside of our comfort zones, to challenge our assumptions, and to embrace new ideas and perspectives. It requires us to collaborate with others, to build coalitions, and to work together towards a common goal.

But the rewards of changing the world are immeasurable. By working together, we can create a world that is more just, equitable, and sustainable. We can build a future where everyone has the opportunity to thrive, where diversity is celebrated, and where the planet is protected for generations to come. The power to change the world lies within each of us. It is up to us to seize that power and use it to create a brighter future for all.

ϷϷϷ

Emotions are the colors of the human experience, painting our lives with joy, sadness, anger, fear, love, and countless other hues. They are our internal compass, guiding us through the complexities of life. Embrace your emotions, learn from them, and use them to connect with others and build meaningful relationships.

EIGHTEEN

WHAT IS THE VALUE OF ART? EXPLORING CREATIVITY AND EXPRESSION.

What is the value of art? This question has been pondered and debated for centuries, with opinions as diverse as the art forms themselves. Art is often seen as a luxury, a frivolous pursuit compared to the practical concerns of life. Yet, throughout history and across cultures, art has held a significant place in society, shaping our understanding of the world, enriching our lives, and offering a unique window into the human spirit. The value of art lies not only in its aesthetic appeal but also in its ability to inspire, provoke, and transform. It is a testament to human creativity, a medium for expression, and a catalyst for social change.

At its core, art is an expression of human creativity. It is the manifestation of our imagination, our emotions, and our unique perspectives on the world. Whether it be a painting, a sculpture, a musical composition, a poem, a dance performance, or a theatrical production, art allows us to transcend the mundane and explore the realms of possibility. It is a testament to our ingenuity, our ability to create something new and meaningful out of raw materials and ideas.

Art provides a powerful medium for self-expression. It allows us to communicate our thoughts, feelings, and experiences in ways that words alone cannot capture. Through art, we can express our joys, sorrows, hopes, and fears. We can share our stories, our dreams, and our visions for the future. Art gives voice to the voiceless, empowers the marginalized, and amplifies the human experience.

Art is not just about self-expression; it is also about communication and connection. It creates a shared experience between the artist and the audience, fostering empathy, understanding, and dialogue. Art can bridge cultural divides, challenge stereotypes, and promote social cohesion. It can create a sense of shared humanity, reminding us that we are all connected by our common experiences, emotions, and aspirations.

Art has the power to inspire and uplift. It can awaken our senses, ignite our imaginations, and touch our hearts. A beautiful painting can transport us to another world, a moving piece of music can evoke deep emotions, and a powerful poem can challenge our perceptions and beliefs. Art can inspire us to be more creative, more compassionate, and more engaged with the world around us.

Art can also provoke and challenge. It can question our assumptions, confront us with uncomfortable truths, and push us to think critically about the world we live in. Art can be a catalyst for social change, sparking conversations, raising awareness, and inspiring action on issues such as inequality, injustice, and environmental degradation.

Art has the ability to transform individuals and communities. It can provide solace in times of grief, hope in times of despair, and joy in times of celebration. Art therapy has been shown to be effective in treating a variety of mental and emotional health conditions, such as depression, anxiety, and trauma. Art can also play a role in education, helping children to develop creativity, critical thinking, and problem-solving skills.

Art is a reflection of our culture and history. It captures the zeitgeist of a particular era, the values, beliefs, and aspirations of a society. By studying art from different periods and cultures, we can gain a deeper understanding of human history, the evolution of societies, and the diversity of human experience.

Art has economic value. It is a multi-billion dollar industry that employs millions of people worldwide. Artists, musicians, actors, writers, and other creative professionals contribute to the economy through their work. Art also attracts tourists, generates revenue for museums and galleries, and enhances the cultural vibrancy of cities and communities.

Art is a form of cultural heritage. It is a legacy that we pass down from one generation to the next. By preserving and protecting works of art, we ensure that future generations can appreciate and learn from the creativity and ingenuity of their ancestors.

The value of art is multifaceted and cannot be measured solely in economic terms. It is a source of beauty, inspiration, expression, communication, and transformation. It enriches our lives, challenges our perceptions, and connects us to something larger than ourselves. Art is a testament to the human spirit, a reminder of our capacity for creativity, compassion, and connection.

ৡৡৡ

Imagination is the spark of creativity, the engine of innovation, and the key to unlocking our full potential. It allows us to transcend the limitations of the present and envision a better future. Embrace your imagination, nurture your creativity, and let your dreams take flight.

NINETEEN

WHY DO WE TELL STORIES? UNDERSTANDING THE POWER OF NARRATIVE.

Why do we tell stories? This question takes us to the heart of human communication, connection, and the very essence of what it means to be human. Stories are not merely forms of entertainment; they are fundamental to our existence, shaping our understanding of the world, ourselves, and our place in it. They are the vessels through which we transmit knowledge, values, and cultural heritage, and they have the power to inspire, transform, and unite us.

From the earliest cave paintings to modern-day novels, films, and video games, storytelling has been an integral part of human civilization. We tell stories to entertain, to educate, to inspire, to warn, to comfort, and to connect with others. Stories are woven into the fabric of our lives, shaping our beliefs, values, and behaviors.

They are the threads that connect us to our past, present, and future.

One of the primary reasons we tell stories is to make sense of the world around us. Stories provide a framework for understanding complex events, emotions, and relationships. They help us interpret our experiences, make sense of our feelings, and find meaning in the chaos of life. Through stories, we can explore different perspectives, challenge our assumptions, and gain new insights into the human condition.

Stories also play a crucial role in transmitting knowledge and cultural heritage. From ancient myths and legends to historical accounts and scientific discoveries, stories have been used to pass down information from one generation to the next. They preserve our collective memory, teach us about our ancestors, and help us understand our place in the world. Stories are not just about the past; they also shape our understanding of the present and our visions for the future.

Stories have the power to inspire and motivate. They can ignite our imaginations, awaken our passions, and challenge us to be better versions of ourselves. Stories of heroes and heroines who overcome adversity can inspire us to face our own challenges with courage and determination. Stories of scientific discoveries and technological breakthroughs can spark our curiosity and encourage us to explore the unknown. Stories of social justice and activism can motivate us to fight for a more equitable and just world.

Stories also provide a source of comfort and solace. In times of grief, loss, or hardship, stories can offer hope, healing, and a sense of connection to others who have experienced similar struggles. They can remind us that we are not alone, that others have faced and overcome adversity, and that there is always the possibility of renewal and growth.

Stories are a powerful tool for building empathy and understanding. By immersing ourselves in the lives of others, whether real or fictional, we can gain a deeper appreciation for different perspectives, experiences, and cultures. Stories can challenge our prejudices, expand our worldview, and foster compassion and empathy for those who are different from us.

The power of narrative lies in its ability to engage our emotions, our imagination, and our intellect. A well-told story can transport us to another time and place, allowing us to experience the world through the eyes of another person. It can make us laugh, cry, fear, and hope. It can challenge our assumptions, expand our horizons, and inspire us to action.

In the digital age, the power of narrative is more important than ever. We are constantly bombarded with information from a variety of sources, making it difficult to discern truth from falsehood, to filter out the noise and focus on what truly matters. Stories can cut through the clutter, capturing our attention, engaging our emotions, and leaving a lasting impression.

Stories have the power to shape public opinion, influence policy decisions, and even spark social movements. The stories we tell ourselves and others about our history, our values, and our aspirations can have a profound impact on the world we create.

As we navigate the complexities of the 21st century, the power of narrative will continue to play a vital role in shaping our understanding of the world and our place in it. By embracing the power of storytelling, we can connect with others, foster empathy and understanding, and create a more just, equitable, and sustainable future for all.

ppp

The future of humanity is a tapestry woven with threads of possibility. It is a story yet to be written, a canvas waiting to be painted. Embrace the unknown, challenge the status quo, and work together to create a more just, equitable, and sustainable world for all.

TWENTY

HOW CAN WE LIVE A MEANINGFUL LIFE? CULTIVATING VALUES AND PURPOSE.

How can we live a meaningful life? This age-old question has echoed through the corridors of philosophy, religion, and personal introspection for centuries. It is a question that speaks to our deepest longings and aspirations, our yearning for a life that is not just lived, but truly felt, valued, and impactful. While the definition of a meaningful life may vary from person to person, there are universal principles and practices that can guide us on this profound journey of self-discovery and fulfillment.

At its core, a meaningful life is one that is lived with intention and purpose. It is a life that is not simply a series of random events but a deliberate creation, a tapestry woven with threads of personal values, passions, and contributions to the world. A meaningful life is not necessarily a life free of challenges or setbacks, but rather one in which those challenges are met with resilience, growth, and a deeper understanding of oneself and the world.

Cultivating values is a crucial step in creating a meaningful life. Values are the guiding principles that shape our choices, our actions, and ultimately, our character. They are the compass that directs us towards a life of integrity, purpose, and fulfillment. Our values can be influenced by our upbringing, our culture, our religious or spiritual beliefs, and our personal experiences. However, it is essential to consciously examine and articulate our values, as they provide a framework for making decisions that align with our deepest beliefs and aspirations.

Some common values that contribute to a meaningful life include honesty, integrity, compassion, kindness, generosity, courage, perseverance, and respect. These values not only guide our interactions with others but also shape our relationship with ourselves. When we live in accordance with our values, we experience a sense of inner peace, satisfaction, and fulfillment.

Purpose is another essential ingredient in a meaningful life. It is the driving force that gives our lives direction, motivation, and significance. Purpose can be found in a variety of ways, from pursuing a fulfilling career to raising a family, from volunteering in our communities to pursuing creative or artistic endeavors. It is not about achieving a specific goal or destination but about embracing a journey of continuous growth, learning, and contribution.

Finding our purpose can be a lifelong process of exploration and self-discovery. It requires us to reflect on our passions, talents, and values. It may involve trying new things, stepping outside of our comfort zones, and taking risks. It may also require us to listen to our intuition, to follow our hearts, and to trust that we are being guided towards a path that is uniquely ours.

Once we have identified our purpose, it is important to integrate it into our daily lives. This can be done through our work, our relationships, our hobbies, or our involvement in our communities. When we live with purpose, we feel a sense of connection to something larger than ourselves, a sense that our lives have meaning and significance.

Living a meaningful life is not just about pursuing our own individual goals and aspirations; it is also about contributing to the well-being of others and the world around us. When we give back to our communities, whether through volunteering, mentoring, or simply acts of kindness, we not only help others but also experience a sense of purpose and fulfillment.

Making a positive impact on the world can take many forms. It can be as simple as offering a helping hand to a neighbor, volunteering at a local shelter, or donating to a worthy cause. It can also involve working towards larger social or environmental goals, such as advocating for social justice, protecting the environment, or promoting peace and understanding.

Living a meaningful life is not always easy. It requires effort, commitment, and a willingness to face challenges and overcome obstacles. But the rewards are immeasurable. When we live with intention, purpose, and values, we experience a sense of inner peace, satisfaction, and fulfillment that cannot be found through material possessions or external validation.

As we navigate the complexities of life, it is important to remember that the journey is just as important as the destination. A meaningful life is not about achieving a certain level of success or happiness; it is about living each day with intention, embracing our passions and values, and making a positive impact on the world. By cultivating our values, discovering our purpose, and contributing to something larger than ourselves, we can create a life that is truly meaningful and fulfilling.

ppp

The journey of life is a quest for meaning and purpose. It is a path filled with challenges, opportunities, and endless possibilities. Embrace the journey, cultivate your values, and discover your unique gifts and talents.

TWENTY-ONE
WHAT IS THE ROLE OF TECHNOLOGY? EXAMINING THE IMPACT OF INNOVATION.

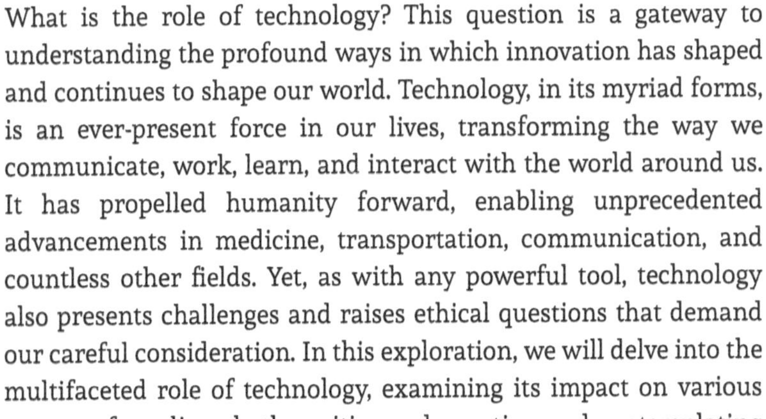

What is the role of technology? This question is a gateway to understanding the profound ways in which innovation has shaped and continues to shape our world. Technology, in its myriad forms, is an ever-present force in our lives, transforming the way we communicate, work, learn, and interact with the world around us. It has propelled humanity forward, enabling unprecedented advancements in medicine, transportation, communication, and countless other fields. Yet, as with any powerful tool, technology also presents challenges and raises ethical questions that demand our careful consideration. In this exploration, we will delve into the multifaceted role of technology, examining its impact on various aspects of our lives, both positive and negative, and contemplating the future of innovation.

At its core, technology is the application of scientific knowledge for practical purposes. It encompasses a vast array of tools, machines, systems, and processes that are designed to solve problems, improve efficiency, and enhance our lives. From the earliest stone tools used by our ancestors to the cutting-edge artificial intelligence systems of today, technology has been a driving force in human evolution and progress.

One of the most significant impacts of technology has been on communication. The advent of the printing press, the telegraph, the telephone, the radio, the television, and the internet has revolutionized the way we connect with each other, transcending geographical boundaries and enabling real-time communication across the globe. Social media platforms, video conferencing tools, and instant messaging apps have further transformed the way we interact, fostering virtual communities and enabling global collaborations.

Technology has also had a profound impact on the workplace. Automation, robotics, and artificial intelligence are reshaping industries, automating tasks, and increasing productivity. While this has led to economic growth and improved efficiency, it has also raised concerns about job displacement and the need for workforce retraining. The rise of the gig economy, fueled by technology platforms, has created new opportunities for flexible work arrangements, but it has also raised questions about workers' rights and protections.

Education has also been transformed by technology. Online learning platforms, educational apps, and virtual reality simulations have expanded access to education, making it more convenient, personalized, and engaging. However, the digital divide, the gap between those who have access to technology and those who do not, remains a significant challenge, particularly in developing countries.

Technology has revolutionized healthcare, leading to breakthroughs in diagnostics, treatment, and disease prevention. Medical imaging technologies, such as MRI and CT scans, have enabled doctors to visualize the inner workings of the human body with unprecedented detail. Robotic surgery has made complex procedures less invasive and more precise. Telemedicine has expanded access to healthcare, particularly for those living in remote or underserved areas. However, the high cost of some technologies and the ethical implications of genetic engineering and other emerging technologies raise important questions about equity and access.

Technology has also transformed the way we consume and interact with information. The internet has become a vast repository of knowledge, accessible to anyone with an internet connection. Search engines, online encyclopedias, and social media platforms have democratized information, empowering individuals to learn, connect, and share ideas. However, the proliferation of fake news, misinformation, and online echo chambers has also raised concerns about the quality and reliability of information in the digital age.

While technology has undoubtedly brought about many positive changes, it also presents a number of challenges and risks. The increasing reliance on technology has raised concerns about privacy, security, and the potential for misuse. Cyberattacks, data breaches, and online surveillance have become major threats in the digital age, highlighting the need for robust cybersecurity measures and ethical guidelines for data collection and use.

The rapid pace of technological change has also raised concerns about the potential for social disruption and inequality. As automation and artificial intelligence continue to advance, there is a risk that certain jobs will become obsolete, leading to unemployment and social unrest. The concentration of wealth and power in the hands of a few tech giants also raises questions about economic inequality and the need for regulatory frameworks to ensure fair competition and protect consumer interests.

As we contemplate the role of technology in our lives, it is important to recognize that it is not a neutral force. Technology is shaped by the values, biases, and interests of those who create and use it. It can be used for good or for ill, to empower or to oppress, to connect or to divide. The future of technology will be determined by the choices we make today.

As responsible citizens, we must engage in critical discussions about the ethical implications of emerging technologies, advocate for policies that promote equity and access, and ensure that technology is used to serve the common good. We must also be mindful of the potential negative impacts of technology and work to mitigate them. By doing so, we can harness the power of innovation to create a more just, equitable, and sustainable future for all.

ϷϷϷ

Technology is a powerful tool that can shape our world for better or for worse. It is a force that can connect us, empower us, and transform our lives. Embrace the possibilities of technology, but be mindful of its potential dangers and use it responsibly.

TWENTY-TWO

WHY DO WE HAVE EMOTIONS? UNDERSTANDING THE ROLE OF FEELINGS.

Why do we have emotions? This fundamental question has intrigued philosophers, scientists, and thinkers for centuries. Emotions are an integral part of the human experience, coloring our lives with joy, sadness, anger, fear, love, and countless other shades of feeling. They shape our perceptions, influence our decisions, and drive our actions. But what is their purpose? Why have we evolved to experience this vast and often tumultuous range of emotions?

In our quest to understand emotions, we must first acknowledge their complexity. Emotions are not simply fleeting sensations; they are complex physiological and psychological responses that involve a symphony of bodily processes, cognitive appraisals, and subjective experiences. When we experience an emotion, our heart rate may quicken, our breathing may change, our muscles may tense, and our brains may release a cascade of neurochemicals. We may also experience a range of thoughts, memories, and associations that further shape our emotional response.

Emotions are not isolated events; they are part of a dynamic and interconnected system that influences our thoughts, behaviors, and relationships. Our emotions can motivate us to act, to connect with others, to protect ourselves, and to pursue our goals. They can also cloud our judgment, lead to impulsive behavior, and create conflict and discord.

The role of emotions in our lives is multifaceted and complex. They serve a variety of functions, both adaptive and maladaptive. One of the primary functions of emotions is to provide us with information about our environment and ourselves. Emotions act as signals, alerting us to potential threats, opportunities, and social cues. They help us navigate complex social interactions, make decisions, and respond to challenges and opportunities.

For example, the emotion of fear alerts us to potential danger, prompting us to flee or fight. The emotion of anger can motivate us to stand up for ourselves and defend our interests. The emotion of sadness can signal loss or disappointment, prompting us to seek comfort and support. The emotion of joy can reinforce positive experiences and motivate us to repeat them.

Emotions also play a crucial role in our social interactions. They help us communicate our needs, desires, and intentions to others. Facial expressions, body language, and vocalizations convey a wealth of emotional information, often more effectively than words alone. Emotions also help us to understand the emotions of others, fostering empathy, connection, and cooperation.

Our emotions are not always rational or helpful. Sometimes they can lead us astray, clouding our judgment and causing us to act in ways that we later regret. For example, fear can lead to irrational phobias, anger can lead to aggression and violence, and sadness can lead to depression and despair.

The challenge of emotional regulation is one that we all face. It is the ability to manage our emotions in healthy and constructive ways, rather than being overwhelmed by them. Emotional regulation involves recognizing our emotions, understanding their triggers, and developing coping mechanisms to manage them effectively. It is a skill that can be learned and honed through practice and self-reflection.

The development of emotional intelligence, the ability to recognize, understand, and manage our own emotions and the emotions of others, is crucial for personal and interpersonal well-being. It allows us to build stronger relationships, navigate social interactions more effectively, and make better decisions.

While emotions can be challenging at times, they are also a source of great joy and enrichment in our lives. They add depth, meaning, and vibrancy to our experiences. They connect us to others, to the world around us, and to our own inner selves. Emotions are what make us human, and they are a gift to be cherished and nurtured.

The question of why we have emotions is a complex one, with no easy answers. But by understanding their role in our lives, we can learn to embrace our emotions, to harness their power, and to use them to create a more fulfilling and meaningful life.

ppp

Emotions are a gift, a window into our inner world, and a compass that guides us through life. They are the essence of our humanity, the colors that paint our experiences, and the fuel that drives our actions. Embrace your emotions, learn from them, and let them enrich your life.

TWENTY-THREE

What is the Power of Imagination? Exploring Creativity and Possibility.

What is the power of imagination? This question invites us to explore the boundless realms of human creativity, innovation, and the potential for personal and societal transformation. Imagination is not merely a frivolous pastime or child's play; it is a fundamental human faculty that shapes our reality, fuels our dreams, and propels us towards new frontiers of possibility. It is the spark that ignites innovation, the catalyst for social change, and the wellspring of artistic expression. In this exploration, we will delve into the multifaceted nature of imagination, examining its role in creativity, problem-solving, empathy, and personal growth, and uncovering the limitless potential it holds for shaping our lives and the world around us.

At its core, imagination is the ability to create mental images, concepts, and scenarios that do not exist in the physical world. It is the faculty of the mind that allows us to transcend the limitations of our senses and experience the world in new and unexpected ways. Imagination is not confined to the realm of fantasy or daydreams; it is an active and dynamic process that involves generating novel ideas, envisioning alternative possibilities, and making connections between seemingly disparate concepts.

Creativity is the lifeblood of imagination. It is the process of bringing something new into existence, whether it be a work of art, a scientific discovery, a technological innovation, or a new way of thinking. Imagination fuels creativity by providing the raw materials for innovation, the spark that ignites new ideas, and the fuel that propels them forward.

Imagination plays a crucial role in problem-solving. When we are faced with a challenge, our imagination allows us to explore different approaches, to think outside the box, and to envision solutions that may not be immediately obvious. It is the ability to see the world from multiple perspectives, to question our assumptions, and to embrace uncertainty.

Imagination is not just about generating new ideas; it is also about empathizing with others. When we read a novel, watch a film, or listen to a story, we are invited to step into the shoes of another person, to see the world through their eyes, and to experience their emotions. This act of imaginative empathy can broaden our understanding of the human experience, foster compassion, and break down barriers between individuals and cultures.

Imagination plays a vital role in personal growth and development. It allows us to envision a better future for ourselves, to set goals, and to overcome obstacles. When we imagine ourselves achieving our dreams, we create a powerful motivator that can propel us forward.

Imagination can also help us cope with adversity, by allowing us to envision alternative scenarios, to find meaning in difficult experiences, and to cultivate hope for the future.

The power of imagination is not limited to individuals; it also has a profound impact on society as a whole. Imagination is the engine of social change, driving innovation, progress, and the evolution of human civilization. It is the force behind scientific breakthroughs, technological advancements, and artistic movements.

Imagination has the power to challenge the status quo, to question authority, and to envision a more just and equitable world. It is the spark that ignites revolutions, the catalyst for social reforms, and the foundation for a more inclusive and compassionate society.

The power of imagination is perhaps most evident in the realm of art. Artists use their imagination to create works that challenge our perceptions, evoke our emotions, and inspire us to think differently about the world. Art can transport us to other worlds, introduce us to new ideas, and challenge our assumptions.

Imagination is not a luxury, but a necessity. It is essential for our survival, our well-being, and our continued progress as a species. In a world that is constantly changing and evolving, imagination allows us to adapt, to innovate, and to create a better future for ourselves and generations to come.

However, the power of imagination is not without its risks. Imagination can be used to manipulate, deceive, and control. It can be harnessed for propaganda, misinformation, and even violence. It is important to cultivate a critical and discerning mind, to question the stories we are told, and to use our imagination in service of truth, justice, and the greater good.

In a world that often seems to prioritize practicality and conformity, it is more important than ever to nurture and cultivate our imagination. By embracing our creative potential, we can unleash the power of possibility, envision a better future, and create a world that is more just, equitable, and sustainable for all.

ԿԿԿ

Imagination is a superpower, a key that unlocks the doors of creativity, innovation, and possibility. It is the birthplace of our dreams, the engine of our aspirations, and the source of our greatest achievements. Embrace your imagination, nurture your creativity, and let your ideas change the world.

TWENTY-FOUR

WHAT IS THE FUTURE OF HUMANITY? IMAGINING WHAT LIES AHEAD.

What is the future of humanity? This question has been asked and pondered by philosophers, scientists, futurists, and ordinary individuals throughout history. It is a question that sparks our imagination, fuels our hopes and fears, and challenges us to envision the possibilities that lie ahead. The future of humanity is a tapestry woven with threads of technological advancement, social change, environmental challenges, and the enduring quest for meaning and purpose.

As we peer into the horizon of the future, one of the most significant forces shaping our destiny is technological advancement. Artificial intelligence, robotics, biotechnology, and nanotechnology are rapidly evolving, promising to transform our lives in unprecedented ways. These technologies have the potential to solve some of our most pressing challenges, such as disease, poverty, and environmental degradation. They could also lead to new forms of creativity, communication, and social interaction.

However, technological progress also raises profound ethical and social questions. Will artificial intelligence surpass human intelligence, and if so, what are the implications for our society? Will robots replace human workers, leading to widespread unemployment and social unrest? Will genetic engineering and other biotechnologies be used to enhance human capabilities, and if so, who will have access to these enhancements? These are questions that we must grapple with as we navigate the uncharted waters of the future.

Another key factor shaping the future of humanity is social change. Our societies are becoming increasingly interconnected and interdependent, as globalization and digital technologies break down traditional barriers and create new opportunities for collaboration and exchange. The rise of social media and other online platforms has given individuals a powerful voice and the ability to connect with others across the globe.

However, social change also brings challenges. Inequality, political polarization, and social unrest are on the rise in many parts of the world. The erosion of trust in traditional institutions and the spread of misinformation and disinformation are fueling social division and conflict. The future of humanity depends on our ability to address these challenges and create a more just, equitable, and inclusive society.

Environmental challenges are another critical factor shaping the future of humanity. Climate change, pollution, and resource depletion pose existential threats to our planet and our way of life. We are already witnessing the devastating effects of climate change, such as rising sea levels, extreme weather events, and the loss of biodiversity. The future of humanity depends on our ability to mitigate these impacts, transition to sustainable practices, and protect the planet for future generations.

Amidst these technological, social, and environmental changes, the enduring quest for meaning and purpose remains a central theme in the human experience. We continue to seek answers to fundamental questions about our existence, our place in the universe, and the meaning of life. As technology advances and our world becomes increasingly complex, the need for meaning and connection becomes even more urgent.

The future of humanity is a story yet to be written. It is a story that will be shaped by our choices, our actions, and our collective will. We have the power to create a future that is bright and hopeful, a future where technology is used to enhance human well-being, where social justice and equality prevail, and where the planet is protected and restored. But we also have the power to create a future that is dark and dystopian, a future where technology is used for control and oppression, where inequality and conflict reign, and where the planet is ravaged by environmental degradation.

The future of humanity is not predetermined. It is a tapestry woven with threads of possibility, shaped by the choices we make today. We can choose to embrace our interconnectedness, to work together to solve global challenges, and to create a more just and sustainable world. Or we can choose to retreat into isolation, to pursue narrow self-interests, and to leave future generations to grapple with the consequences of our inaction.

The choice is ours. The future of humanity rests in our hands.

ppp

The future of humanity is a blank canvas, waiting for us to paint our vision of a better world. It is a call to action, a challenge to create a more just, equitable, and sustainable society. Embrace the future with hope, courage, and a commitment to making a positive impact on the world.

TWENTY-FIVE
SUMMARY

In our exploration of life's big questions, we've embarked on a journey through the realms of philosophy, science, and the human experience. We've pondered the nature of reality, grappling with the elusive concept of what is truly real. We've delved into the depths of our own being, seeking to understand the essence of our identity and the forces that shape who we are. We've contemplated the meaning and purpose of our existence, exploring the various paths that can lead to a fulfilling and meaningful life.

Our journey has taken us through the complex terrain of morality, where we've wrestled with questions of right and wrong, fairness, and equality. We've examined the role of society, recognizing the importance of communities and cultures in shaping our values, beliefs, and behaviors. We've contemplated the wonders of nature, appreciating its beauty and recognizing our interconnectedness with the environment.

We've pondered the vastness and mystery of the universe, tracing its origins back to the Big Bang and exploring the forces that continue to shape its evolution. We've considered the power of technology to transform our world, both for better and for worse, and the importance of using it responsibly and ethically.

We've delved into the depths of human emotion, seeking to understand the role of feelings in our lives, from love and joy to fear and sadness. We've celebrated the power of imagination, recognizing its role in creativity, problem-solving, empathy, and personal growth. We've contemplated the future of humanity, envisioning the possibilities that lie ahead as we navigate the challenges and opportunities of the 21st century.

Throughout this journey, we've encountered complex and multifaceted questions with no easy answers. We've learned that the pursuit of knowledge is an ongoing process, a lifelong journey of exploration and discovery. We've discovered that our understanding of the world is shaped by our own unique perspectives, experiences, and beliefs.

As we continue to explore life's big questions, we must embrace our curiosity, our open-mindedness, and our willingness to learn. We must be willing to challenge our assumptions, to consider different viewpoints, and to engage in respectful dialogue with others. We must strive to live our lives with intention, purpose, and values, seeking to make a positive impact on the world around us.

The journey of self-discovery and understanding is a never-ending one. It is a journey that can lead us to a deeper appreciation for the world and our place in it, a greater sense of purpose and meaning, and a more fulfilling and authentic life. As we continue to explore life's big questions, we open ourselves up to the endless possibilities that lie ahead, embracing the challenges and opportunities that come our way.

The questions we have explored are not merely academic exercises; they are fundamental to our existence. By engaging with these questions, we deepen our understanding of ourselves, our relationships, and the world around us. We become more informed citizens, more compassionate individuals, and more active participants in shaping the future.

In the end, the quest for knowledge is not just about finding answers; it is about asking the right questions. It is about embracing the mystery and wonder of life, the beauty and complexity of the world, and the infinite potential that lies within each of us. It is about living a life that is both meaningful and fulfilling, a life that is guided by our values, our passions, and our unwavering commitment to the pursuit of truth, justice, and the greater good.

Citation And References

This book represents the culmination of extensive research and meticulous analysis, incorporating a diverse range of sources, including numerous books, scholarly studies, and personal experiences. Additionally, I have scoured various websites to gather relevant information and data essential for the compilation of this work. I have taken every precaution to ensure the accuracy of the information presented and have diligently cited all sources to acknowledge their contributions.

Despite these efforts, the possibility of inadvertent errors remains. I deeply value the insights of my readers and appreciate any feedback that can help identify and rectify such inaccuracies. I encourage you to bring any discrepancies to my attention.

Your feedback is not only welcome but crucial, as it will aid in correcting current editions and enhancing the content of future ones. I am committed to maintaining the highest standards of accuracy and reliability in my work and thank you for your support and understanding.

Additionally, I firmly uphold the principle of freedom of speech and expression as guaranteed under Article 19(1)(a) of the Constitution of India, and I respect the diverse viewpoints and expressions of all readers.

ᑭᑭᑭ

Other Books Of The Author

1. Empowering Minds: A Journey into Women's Self-Discovery and Power
2. The Dynamics of Motivation: Catalyzing Thought into Action
3. Meditation and Mental Well Being: The Path to Inner Peace and Clarity
4. The Psychology of Child Education: Nurturing Future Generations
5. Ethical Enlightenment: A Modern Guide to Living with Integrity
6. Voices of Empowerment: Stories of Women Rising Against Odds
7. Social Psychology in Everyday Life: Understanding Human Connections
8. The Essence of Motivational Speaking: Inspiring Change in Others
9. Balancing Acts: Women, Work, and the Will to Lead
10. Guiding with Grace: Raising Children with Compassion and Awareness
11. The Power of Positive Aging: Embracing Life After Fifty
12. Building Resilient Communities: Social Work in Action
13. The Ethical Educator: Principles for Teaching and Learning
14. From Insight to Impact: Social Psychology for a Better World
15. The Ethics of Empathy: A Guide to Ethical Living
16. The Science of Empowering the Self: Navigating Life's Challenges with Psychological Wisdom
17. The Mindful Conscious Leader: Meditation Techniques for Modern Management
18. Pioneering Spirit: Women's Pathways to Leadership and Empowerment
19. Feeling to Healing: The Role of Emotional Intelligence in Child Development
20. Transformative Talks and Words of Inspiration: Insights into Motivational Oratory

Bhajan
101. Pilgrimage of the Soul: Spiritual Journeys in India

❦❦❦

Contact

Dr. Minakshi Bansal
Social Activist
Ahmedabad, Gujarat, Bharat
minakshiindiag20@yahoo.com

❦❦❦

|| LOKAHA SAMASTHAHA SUKHINO BHAVANTU ||

www.ingramcontent.com/pod-product-compliance
Lightning Source LLC
Chambersburg PA
CBHW020538160726
47991CB00002B/486